Praise for *The Master Key*

Thanks for placing *The Master Key System* in the hands! The teachings of Charles Haanel helped change the direction of my life. Thanks so much...

—Genia Rodgers

We never understood why one day could be so wonderful and the next day be so lousy, but now we do. This book is giving us a great experience in self-development. We now know we have always possessed the power to take ourselves where we wanted to go and this book gives us the how-to. Thanks for reviving *The Master Key System*—it is a valuable tool.

—Howard & Lisa McCoy

We just received this morning our copy of *The Master Key System* by Charles F. Haanel which we ordered through Amazon.com. I opened it at random and began reading and was immediately seized by the depth and profundity of the author's words. I don't know what I was expecting, but this is FAR, FAR more. My wife and I have been reading aloud and discussing passages all morning quite forgetting our normal work. To say we read with delight tells only half the story as the book is also deeply challenging and one might even say, awesome in it's implications. We only put the book down to order four more copies which we would like to share with family and close friends. Thank you for the magnificent job you have done in bringing this great work to a wider public. Our appreciation is immense. Thank you again for your service.

—Peter S. Sumner
Fremantle, Western Australia

This book is something of a classic in the world of mind-stuff and I would consider it a "must read" for any student of self-improvement. I found myself reading the Haanel book for the third time and like *Think and Grow Rich* and *You Were Born Rich*, it's the kind of material that one can read every year and still get a refreshing new viewpoint along with a great lesson to take control of your life!

—Charles Umphred
VP of Marketing, Scentsations, Inc.

Praise for *Master Key Arcana*

I just received my copy of *Master Key Arcana*. This book is sure to become a classic. The content of the book is tremendous. Thanks...

—Andrew M.

In this new volume a deeper understanding of Haanel's ideas is rounded out with the final Parts 25 to 28. Readers of *The Master Key* who may have sensed a certain "unfinished" quality are now finally satisfied. Also included in this volume is an excellent 3-part summary of The Master Key in Haanel's own words. The Master Key Psychological Chart is (with a few adjustments) still useful. The history buff and antiquarian will enjoy the Images of Original Material complete with pictures which concludes this eminently practical and inspiring sequel to Charles Haanel's The Master Key.

This is yet another stimulating and thought-provoking publication from Kallisti Publishing. It's a good read, too; and a book well worthy to merit many dog-eared pages.

—L.J. Schnierer
Largesse Associates

Praise for
The Amazing Secrets of the Yogi

I became interested in yoga a couple of years ago and have gone to classes, retreats, read books, etc. This is one of the more interesting books I have read on the topic of yoga.

I love that it really explores the power of breath and discusses techniques to harness prana. Many recent books tend to skim over this aspect of yoga, but Haanel really devoted himself to this very powerful practice. He also explained the eight aspects of yoga and how they combine to form a powerful way of life.

I recommend this book to those who want a deeper insight into yoga, its background, and its practice. Although it sometimes comes across as dated, I feel it has a wealth of information not readily found in many recent yoga books. Definitely worth the price!

—K. Lykes

THE MASTER KEY WORKBOOK

Anthony R. Michalski
&
Robert Schmitz

Kallisti Publishing
Wilkes-Barre, PA 18702

Published by
Kallisti Publishing, 332 Center Street, Wilkes-Barre, PA, 18702

FIRST EDITION

Other fine books published by Kallisti Publishing are available from your local bookstore or direct from the publisher.

ISBN 0-9761111-1-X

Kallisti Publishing
332 Center Street, Wilkes-Barre, PA 18702
Phone (877) 444-6188 • Fax (419) 781-1907
www.kallistipublishing.com

About the Authors

Anthony R. Michalski (AKA "Tony") is the owner and the chief cook and bottle washer of Kallisti Publishing. Begun in 2000, Kallisti Publishing first published *The Master Key System* by Charles F. Haanel, which was received with wide acclaim. Following on that success, Tony published more books by other great authors and he continues to bring Haanel's other books to bookstores near you.

Tony received a BA from The Pennsylvania State University and a Ph.D. from the School of Hard Knocks, has worked too many jobs to list, and has owned a couple of businesses. Along the way, he ballroom danced, fixed computers, played guitar, was a President and Area Governor in Toastmasters International, and wrote articles for a weekly news magazine in his area.

When he is not working on a new book, which is rare, Tony enjoys travelling to New York City, cooking, talking politics, listening to and playing music, and reading. (That last one is shocking considering that he is a publisher!)

To contact Tony, you can call Kallisti Publishing or E-mail him at *tony@kallistipublishing.com*. He is also a frequent poster at Kallisti Publishing's Message Board.

" "My life has been proof that the principles that Charles Haanel teaches are totally true and correct. We need to educate the masses about the truth of who we are and how powerful an effect our thoughts have on our lives."

Robert "Bob" Schmitz was born in New York City and attended college at the University of Dayton in Ohio. Two endeavors drastically altered his life: He read *Think & Grow Rich* and he studied a success course that was produced by the "Success Motivation Institute."

At 30, Bob bought a convenience store franchise. He was eventually elected to a leadership position to represent other store owners within the company. In the early 80's, Bob opened one of the first video rental stores on Long Island. When that became a tremendous success, Bob sold his stores and moved to Florida to pursue his own personal mental and spiritual growth.

In late 1987, Bob began another business marketing skin and hair care products. He developed a nationwide business over the next four years and incorporated training programs using what he learned about self-mastery. This lead to his famous "Mindset to Millionaire" seminars, which impelled many people to levels of excellence of which they had only dreamed. (Soon to be available from Kallisti Publishing!)

Bob moved to Pennsylvania in 2003 to build a specialized candle business with good friends. The company has been experiencing amazing growth. Bob is also an accomplished artist. His art can be viewed at *www.bobschmitz.com*.

Thank you...

Tony wishes to thank... Mom, Dad, Katrina, Charlie, Schmitty, Charles F. Haanel, the legion of seekers who made *The Master Key System* the success that it is, the American Free Enterprise System, and God.

Finding who to thank for support and influence in my life is easy. I will mention only those who have had a direct or indirect influence in attracting me to the point of becoming involved in my study of "The Master Key."

First, nothing is possible without the Universal Mind, my Higher Power, one word name— "God."

I have to thank the great authors from whom I garnered great insights: the late Napoleon Hill for his book *Think & Grow Rich*; Maxwell Maltz, author of *Psycho-Cybernetics*; Dr. Joseph Murphy, author of *The Power of the Subconscious Mind*; Dr. Wayne Dyer and all of his books; Deepak Chopra and his books and tapes; Anthony Robbins; The Landmark Organization and their self-awareness training; Bob Proctor; Vernon Howard and *The Mystic Path to Cosmic Power*; and Brian Tracey and *The Psychology of Success*.

I want to thank Bill and Bob for your desire to find a better way and for influencing so many of us who were lost. I want to thank Rose Joya from the "Imagineering" workshop for opening my mind to recognize that we create our lives from our dominant thoughts. I practiced Yoga with Pat Byrum at her ashram on the water in Stuart, Florida—thank you for the great knowledge.

Certain people come into our lives for an important reason. At the time, we don't know what that reason is until one day, we look back and we realize why. One of them is Bill Bampton who, in 1995, passed on information to me which led to the teachings of Charles Haanel. Another is Charles Umphred, who introduced me to Tony. Without Tony, this book would not have been written and arranged at this time and in this manner. Another person is Bobby Scocozzo, without whose persistence, love, friendship, and belief in me at a time when I really needed it, influenced me to come to Northeast Pennsylvania, where I became involved with Tony and "The Master Key." My true friends, George Bernier and Mark Wilten in Atlanta; Vince Martin in Baltimore; and my brother, Leo Perlmutter, in New York, who came through at the turning point in my life and again showed me that we are all connected in Universal Mind and that the Law of Vibration attracts those of like vibration to you when the time is right. It has attracted a Happy Hippy to me, who has shown me that life can be filled with love, and that humor, cheerfulness, and a loving attitude can get you through anything..

I also wish to mention Noelle Kim, a person who had a great influence over me in my quest for truth and who was my partner in the *Mindset To Millionaire Seminars*. I cannot fail to mention my cousin, Tom Woods, who was my publisher and partner in the "Mindset" seminars and tapes and helped get the word out during those challenging times.

Thanks to those I have not mentioned. I hope you all get to study the teachings of this workbook and most definitely practice the exercises. I believe strongly that this is the fast-track to self-mastery and blissful happiness. Remember, "If you shoot for the stars, it will seem easy to rise above the clouds."

Bob Schmitz
October, 2004

Table of Contents

Though an inheritance of acres may be bequeathed, an inheritance of knowledge and wisdom cannot. The wealthy man may pay others for doing his work for him, but it is impossible to get his thinking done for him by another, or to purchase any kind of self-culture.

—Samuel Smiles (1812-1904)

Introduction

Writing, designing, and publishing *The Master Key Workbook* has been quite a journey. For years, just about since I began to publish *The Master Key System* in 2000, people have asked me about a workbook to go along with it. Folks wanted something that would add to *The Master Key System* and something they could use in a work group setting.

The idea is a good one, of course, and also an obvious one. What better to accompany *The Master Key System* than a workbook? Thus, the idea was implanted in the back of my mind. The real question became: How does one make a good workbook?

I am probably a lot like you. I have attended a bunch of seminars; I've read tons of books; I've worked with and written inside of many workbooks. Some workbooks just plain sucked. (Excuse my loose language there, but there really is no other way to phrase that.) They were boring, redundant, simplistic, and uninspiring. I hated them. I actually got one at a very big name seminar. Boy, was I disappointed with that one!

Some workbooks were good. They added to the original text on which they were based. They had good exercises that were fun and enlightening. They made me actually work! That's good because then I actually got something form the workbook. Those books made me happy. Unfortunately, there are not too many of them.

One thing I did notice is that I never read or completed a great workbook. Like *The Master Key System* is a great book or *Think & Grow Rich* is a great book, I have never once read or worked with a great workbook. Like I stated, I've done good ones, but nothing great. Not one book that stood on its own while adding to the original body. Not one where the exercises really made me stretch. Not one that elevated me.

I was moved to change that. I wanted to make a truly great workbook. As Steve Jobs would keep saying when they were making the first Macintosh computer, I wanted this workbook to be *"insanely great!"*

I wanted it to be used as an addition to *The Master Key System* or as in introduction to it; as a fun and inspiring method to self-mastery or as an intensive and serious way to self-discipline. In other words, I wanted a workbook that could actually be used by an individual, however that individual desired to use it: either as a quick review or as an intensive training.

Bob Schmitz laid the groundwork for the *Workbook* as you see it. He has been training people in mind stuff for many years and many of the exercises that you will do in this book are exercises that Bob has been doing with students for years. They are quite powerful. Bob also added many of the insights that appear in this books that endeavour to explain Haanel's original words. This book would not have been possible without Bob.

Once Bob supplied the original outline, which he obtained from teaching the stuff for so long, I applied the layout and design and cherry-picked the best of the best from all the different sources at my disposal. It was difficult, to say the least. I wanted each Week to build on the next, just like Haanel, without interfering with Haanel's exercises. Like I said, it was a challenge.

When I thought that I had accomplished that, it was time to test it. It was time to put it to work.

Introduction

I did the *Workbook*. Bob did it. I had a few other people go through the *Workbook*, too. I had everyone, including myself, put notes in the *Workbook*, make corrections, insert suggestions, and anything else that came to mind.

The result is the book you now hold in your hands. It is tested and ready for general use. I really do not expect this book to be a big seller. (I know. It's a terrible thing to say and think, but I have my reasons, which I will outline here.) It asks for a person to do some pretty serious work and soul-searching. I have found that people like soda-pop books and workbooks, those that have a lot of pop and sizzle and give you a good sugar rush, but really offer no long term knowledge or benefits. (I will not mention any names here. You know who the guilty are.)

The people who actually want to succeed and practice self-improvement are few; most merely mouth words and want to "feel" like they are doing something. This is not meant to be sad or pessimistic. On the contrary, it is to be expected. It is neither good nor bad, it merely is. Thus, *The Master Key Workbook* was written, compiled, and designed with the true seeker and practitioner in mind. If you work at it and strive for it, success can be yours. With *The Master Key Workbook*, you will read a lot, do many invigorating exercises, and explore yourself more than you ever have. It is my hope, though, that you will benefit in many ways.

I see this Workbook as being something that you review at least once per year. Perhaps you'll take the time to do an annual review of yourself. The first time you do *The Master Key Workbook*, though, take your time if you are doing it by yourself. Read something over and over until you thoroughly understand it. You are not in a race to the finish; even if you were, it's a race of endurance and persistence, not speed. If you are part of a study group, ask questions when you need to and discuss every concept thoroughly. Help each other and share. It's very amazing that the sharing of ideas and experiences emboldens everyone who hears them.

Above all, enjoy the journey. Like Haanel says, "Life is an unfoldment, not an accretion." If something is giving you trouble, then step from it for a few days. You own the Workbook; it does not own you. Learning is fun and exciting, but real learning can be tough and painful. It can be important to take a break when you feel it is necessary. It is even more important, though, to carry on and see the thing through. Make certain of that and all will fall into place.

Please enjoy this work, this labour of love, this fantastic journey. I sincerely hope that you attain everything that you desire. I hope that this books helps you to do that. In the end, though, it is most important to remember that you did it! While this book may be a meager map, you, my friend are the true discoverer.

Have fun...

Tony Michalski
Wilkes-Barre, PA
October, 2004

How to Use This Book

You will get a lot from this book. Hopefully, the seeds of success that are within you will become watered enough to sprout roots and break through the soil into the light of day and you will spread your leaves and petals wide for all to see and admire. In order for that to occur, this *Workbook* must be used properly. Here are a few guidelines and tips to help you get the most from this book.

Use this book in conjunction with *The Master Key System*.
Yes, this book can be used on its own, but it was written with the idea that you would have a copy of *The Master Key System* and that you would read both the *Master Key Workbook* and *The Master Key System* together.

Work slowly.
There is no need to rush things. This is a race of endurance, not speed.

Work diligently.
Nothing beats patient and persistent work. Perhaps you've seen on a restaurant's menu "Good cooking takes time." Well, the same goes for self-improvement. You will get to where you are going as long as you keep at it.

Complete the book once.
There is nothing as important as completing what one begins.

Do the book in order the first time.
Haanel paced *The Master Key System* perfectly. This book is based on that pacing. It will do well for you to progress through the book in the order given rather than jumping from section to section. Each exercise builds on the previous one. Completing them in order will make sense.

Review the book on an annual basis.
When you do your personal evaluation, take the time to review this book. You will be able to track how your goals changed or how you progressed in advancement toward your goals. It is important that you do this. Persistence is one of the most important things that you can practice.

Do the exercises!
When you are requested to write something, actually write something. Do not make a mental note and then move to the next part. You will be wasting your time. Writing is setting your thoughts onto paper, making them permanent in a way. Writing helps to crystallize thoughts and make them stronger. Please do so. The other exercises should be attacked the same way: with purpose and diligence. You will only get from the *Workbook* what you put into it.

Get coaching.
Hopefully, you will be able to go through this book with a group or someone who can help you to completely understand all of the concepts. A good partner or group also motivates you to do all of the exercises to the best of your ability. If you are unable to find a group, Kallisti Publishing offers one-on-one coaching (*www.masterkeycoaching.com*) and a Message Board, where your questions will be answered by a community of seekers like yourself (*www.kallistipublishing.com*).

Have fun!
That is by far the most important guideline. Relax, enjoy yourself, and enjoy the journey.

Charles F. Haanel
(May 22, 1866 - November 27, 1949)

Charles F. Haanel was born in Ann Arbor, Michigan on May 22, 1866. He received many degrees, including hon. Ph.D., College National Electronic Institute; Metaphysics, Psy. D., College of Divine Metaphysics; and M.D., Universal College of Dupleix, India. He is the ex-President of the Continental Commercial Company and the ex-President of the Sacramento Valley Improvement Company.

He is the author of works on philosophy, psychology, causation, science of living, personality, and science of mind, synthesized in *The Master Key System*, a system of philosophy for application to the affairs of everyday life.

Mr. Haanel was affiliated with many groups, including Fellow London College of Psychotherapy; member Authors' League of America; American Society of Psychical Research; member of the Society of Rosicrucians; the American Suggestive Therapeutical Association; Science League of America; Pi Gamma Mu Fraternity; Master Mason, Keystone Lodge No. 243, A.F. & A.M.; created a Noble in Moolah Temple.

Mr. Haanel died on November 27, 1949 at the age of 83. He was buried in Bellefontaine Cemetery, St. Louis.

Nan-in, a Japanese master during the Meiji era (1868-1912), received a university professor who came to inquire about Zen.

Nan-in served tea. He poured his visitor's cup full, and then kept on pouring.

The professor watched the overflow until he no longer could restrain himself. "It is over-full. No more will go in!"

"Like this cup," Nan-in said, "you are full of your own opinions and speculations. How can I show you Zen unless you first empty your cup?"

—"A Cup of Tea" from
Zen Flesh, Zen Bones

Week One

An Introduction to The Master Key System

The Letter of Transmittal

It is my privilege to enclose herewith Week One of The Master Key System. Would you bring into your life more power? Get the power consciousness. More health? Get the health consciousness. More happiness? Get the happiness consciousness. Live the spirit of these things until they become yours by right. It will then become impossible to keep them from you. The things of the world are fluid to a power within man by which he rules them.

You need not acquire this power. You already have it. But you want to understand it; you want to use it; you want to control it; you want to impregnate yourself with it, so that you can go forward and carry the world before you.

Day by day, as you go on and on, as you gain momentum, as your inspiration deepens, as your plans crystallize, as you gain understanding, you will come to realize that this world is no dead pile of stones and timber, but that it is a living thing! It is made up of the beating hearts of humanity. It is a thing of life and beauty.

It is evident that it requires understanding to work with material of this description. But those who come into this understanding are inspired by a new light—a new force. They gain confidence and greater power each day. They realize their hopes and their dreams come true. Life has a deeper, fuller, clearer meaning than before.

The world without is a reflection of the world within. ***The Main Points***

All possession is based on consciousness.

The individual is related to the objective world by the objective mind. The brain is the organ of this mind.

He is related to the Universal Mind by the subconscious mind. The Solar Plexus is the organ of this mind.

The Universal Mind is the life principle of every atom that is in existence.

The ability of the individual to think is his ability to act upon the Universal and bring it into manifestation.

The result of this action and interaction is cause and effect; every thought is a cause and every condition an effect.

Harmonious and desirable conditions are obtained by right thinking.

Discord, inharmony, lack, and limitation are the result of wrong thinking.

The source of all power is the world within, the Universal Fountain of Supply, the Infinite Energy of which each individual is an outlet.

Select a room where you can be alone and undisturbed. Sit erect, comfortably, but do not lounge. Let your thoughts roam where they will, but be perfectly still for fifteen minutes to half an hour. Continue this for three or four days or for a week until you secure full control of your physical being. ***The Exercise***

The Tale of the Elephant

In India, elephants are used for manual labor. When the elephant is small and weighs approximately 200 pounds, it is securely tied with a heavy-duty rope. In between "jobs," the elephant often tries to break through its bonds. The calf whines, tugs, and even tries to chew through the rope; but it is unable to break free. Finally, the elephant gives up. He accepts his circumstances. His spirit is broken. The elephant believes there is absolutely no chance to free himself and overcome his "limitation."

This is recognized as a "defining moment." A defining moment is the exact moment one adopts and/or accepts a new belief that drastically alters his life. He accepts this "new belief" as a "truth," regardless if it is true or not. Because the brain accepts repetition of thought and deduction as "the truth," the rope reigns sovereign not only in the calf's immediate environment, but in his mind as well.

With this "belief" deeply embedded in the elephant's mind, his handler came up with an ingenious idea to permanently disempower him. He realized all that was needed was to tie the four-ton animal up with extremely small ropes and he would remain tied. In the elephant's mind, any size rope would keep him "securely" confined.

You are not an elephant! Rise up and break through the confining ropes in your mind. When you're faced with change, change your perspective. When you're overwhelmed with something new, change your view.

Your Mental Attitude

All experiences in life are the result of our habitual or predominant mental attitude. The reason some get more and others less is not because of greed or good luck, but because some have an attitude of lack and others an attitude of abundance. **The world within is a reflection of the world without.** What comes to us in the world without is what we already possess in the world within.

This is not new. You always had this power. If the effects in your life are not to your liking, change the nature of your thoughts to focus on what you want instead of what you don't want.

Everything we have in life is a result of our consciousness.

All of the lessons and all of the exercises in this book are geared towrd changing how you think, because how you think and what you think determine what you have in your life. That idea will be repeated again and again in order for you to not only understand it, but to internalize it.

The secret of all power, all achievement, and all possession depends upon our method of thinking.

Let's begin here by identifying our "ropes"—those things that mentally hold us in bondage. How do you see yourself right now at this moment? Think carefully and be painfully honest. Only by facing the truth and knowing the truth can we progress.

List some obstacles, barriers, or limitations that you believe are preventing you from achieving complete success in any area of your life.

1. My age
2. Effort wont pay off.
3. Failure resulting in financial insecurity
4. Being unsure ~~itisof~~ what I really want to do
5.
6.
7.
8.
9.
10.
11.
12.
13.
14.
15.
16.
17.
18.
19.
20.

*The Universal
Mind and You*

Harmony in the world within means the ability to control our thoughts and to determine for ourselves how any experience is to affect us. We are related to the world without by the **Objective Mind**. The brain is the physical organ of this mind.

We are related to the world within by the **Subconscious Mind**. The solar plexus is the organ of this mind. This system of nerves presides over all subjective sensations, such as joy, fear, love, anger, and imagination.

The **Universal Mind** is that consciousness pervading the entire universe, occupying all space and being the same in kind in every point of existence. It is all powerful, all wisdom, and always present. It is all in all.

Through the Subconscious Mind we are connected to Universal Mind, and in this way we are brought into relation with the infinite constructive forces of the Universe.

Your consciousness is part of Universal Consciousness like a drop of water is part of the ocean. It is like in kind, but it is not "the ocean." The consciousness that focuses in your brain cells is the same consciousness that focuses in the brain cells of everyone else. Each one of us is but an individualization of the Universal.

The world within is the cause, the world without is the effect. To change the effect you must change the cause. Most people attempt to change effects by working with effects. They keep repeating the same mistakes over and over again. The effects—or the focusing of thoughts on the effects—keep producing more of the same effects.

Understanding this gives us the power to control the effects in our lives. By substituting abundance for poverty, health for sickness, wisdom for ignorance, harmony for discord, and freedom for tyranny, we create the outcomes in our lives that we want and desire.

Recognition

The world within is the universal fountain of supply. The world without is the outlet of that stream. **Our ability to receive depends upon our recognition of this Universal Fountain.** This recognition is a mental process.

We live in a fathomless sea of plastic mind substance that is ever alive and active. It takes form according to our mental demand. Thought forms the mold that will be expressed in our lives. Thought, therefore, becomes reality.

As our recognition of this process grows, we will better be able to control the outcomes in our lives and attain the things we want.

A Key Point

> **By being truthful about yourself and therefore knowing yourself, you begin the path to success and achievement. By keeping your attention on the things you want rather than the things you do not want, you condition yourself to attain success and achievement.**

When practicing *the exercise*, notice how the fingers twitch, the nose tickles, the foot taps, and the leg jerks, or whatever "unconscious" movements your body does. Your body is your instrument—your possession—yet one finds it to be one of the most difficult things to control! Why is this?

We must bring ourselves into a recognition of where we are. Bringing into focus our own body is the first step to breaking through those perceptions. You learn how to focus and bring your mind from wasted effort and into the all-important *Now*.

It is imperative that you master this lesson. By bringing your body into focus, you will be on your way to mastering your mind.

Practicing the Exercise

Write Your Impressions Here

"This above all: To thine own self be true,
And it must follow, as the night the day,
Thou canst not then be false to any
man."

—William Shakespeare, *Hamlet*

Week Two

The Basics of Your Mind

The Letter of Transmittal

Our difficulties are largely due to confused ideas and ignorance of our true interests. The great task is to discover the laws of nature to which we are to adjust ourselves. Clear thinking and moral insight are, therefore, of incalculable value. All processes, even those of thought, rest on solid foundations.

The keener the sensibilities, the more acute the judgment, the more delicate the taste, the more refined the moral feelings, the more subtle the intelligence, the loftier the aspiration—the purer and more intense are the gratifications which existence yields. Hence, it is that the study of the best that has been thought in the world gives supreme pleasure.

The powers, uses, and possibilities of the mind under the new interpretations are incomparably more wonderful than the most extravagant accomplishment, or even dreams of material progress. Thought is energy. Active thought is active energy; concentrated thought is concentrated energy. Thought concentrated on a definite purpose becomes power. This is the power which is being used by those who do not believe in the virtue of poverty, or the beauty of self-denial. They perceive that this is the talk of weaklings.

The ability to receive and manifest this power depends upon the ability to recognize the Infinite Energy ever dwelling in man, constantly creating and recreating his body and mind, and ready at any moment to manifest through him in any needful manner. In exact proportion to the recognition of this truth will be the manifestation in the outer life of the individual.

Week Two explains the method by which this is accomplished.

The conscious and subconscious are the two modes of mental activity. **The Main Points**

Ease and perfection depend entirely upon the degree in which we cease to depend upon the conscious mind.

The value of the subconscious is enormous: It guides us, it warns us, it controls the vital processes, and it is the seat of memory.

The conscious mind has the faculty of discrimination; it has the power of reasoning; it is the seat of the will and may impress the subconscious.

"Conscious mind is reasoning will. Subconscious mind is instinctive desire, the result of past reasoning will."

To impress the subconscious, mentally state what is wanted.

If the desire is in harmony with the forward movement of the great Whole, forces will be set in motion which will bring about the result.

Our environment reflects conditions corresponding to the predominant mental attitude which we entertain.

The Law of Attraction states that our environment reflects our predominant mental attitude.

Thought is a creative energy, and will automatically correlate with its object and bring it into manifestation.

This time you will begin to control your thought. Always take the same **The Exercise** room, the same chair, and the same position, if possible. In some cases it is not convenient to take the same room. In this case simply make the best use of such conditions as may be available. Now be perfectly still as before, but inhibit all thought. This will give you control over all thoughts of care, worry, and fear, and will enable you to entertain only the kind of thoughts you desire. Continue this exercise until you gain complete mastery.

The Two Parts of the Mind

There are two parts of the mind: **the Conscious mind and the Subconscious mind.**

The **Conscious Mind** is the center of perception, analysis, judgement, and operates through the five physical senses.

The **Subconscious Mind**, besides its work on the mental plane, controls the regular functions which make physical life possible.

We use the Conscious Mind more when we are first learning something new. Once we have developed the skill through repetition, the Subconscious, which controls memory and runs the show, takes over. **The Subconscious is the seat of habit.**

The value of the Subconscious is enormous. It warns us; it furnishes us with names and facts; and provides scenes from the storehouse of memory. It accomplishes intricate tasks that the Conscious mind has inability to do.

Directing the Subconscious Mind

The Conscious mind can direct the Subconscious Mind. This is how you can turn your life around and reverse negative conditions and create positive ones. Since the Subconscious takes instruction from the Conscious, it cannot argue the instructions. If it has accepted wrong suggestions, the sure method of overcoming them is by using a strong counter-suggestion repetitiously. Since the Subconscious is creative and one with Universal Mind, it will at once create the freedom suggested.

The Conscious Mind is reasoning will. The Subconscious Mind is instinctive desire. The Conscious Mind engages in analysis and proving, the Subconscious Mind perceives by intuition. Hence its processes are rapid. It never sleeps or rests. It has been found that by simply stating to the Subconscious Mind certain specific things to be accomplished, forces are set into operation that lead to the desired result. If you learn to command your Subconscious, infinite resources are at your command.

> **Our environment reflects conditions corresponding to the predominant mental attitude which we entertain.**
>
> **This is known as the Law of Attraction.**

Rewriting Your Story

There is a thinking stuff from which all things are made and which, in its original state, permeates and fills the interspaces of the universe. A thought in this substance produces the thing that is imaged by the thought. A person can form things in his thought and by impressing his thought upon formless substance can cause the thing he thinks about to be created.

Begin to work on your Subconscious today. In **Week One,** you were to write a list of the things that you perceived were impeding you from living a successful life (your "ropes"). Here, you are to write an affirmation to counteract those perceived limitations. For example, if you wrote "I have no money," write as an affirmation "I am wealthy."

My Affirmations

1. I am youthful

2. My effort will pay off

3. My success will result in financial security

4. I'm sure I want to do things, and it will lead to other things I want to do.

5.

6.

7.

8.

9.

Recite your affirmations daily when you awaken each morning and before you fall asleep each night and at quiet moments during the day. Any limitations that you have defined are just excuses to keep you from achieving complete success. Once you take complete responsibility for your life you will realize that you have the power to create your life by choosing your beliefs, thoughts, feeling, and actions.

Words to Live By

Those who say it cannot be done should not interrupt the person doing it.

—Chinese Proverb

Life is a grindstone. Whether it grinds you down or polishes you up depends on what you're made of.

—Jacob M. Braude

Sometimes when I consider what tremendous consequences come from little things, I am tempted to think there are no little things.

—Bruce Barton

We are what we repeatedly do. Excellence, then, is not an act, but a habit.

—Aristotle

Whether you think you can or you think you can't—you are right.

—Henry Ford

Anything the mind can conceive and believe, it can achieve

—Napoleon Hill

In this section, we learn that the Subconscious mind is controlled and influenced by the Conscious mind. We receive data from our five senses; that data is processed and filtered by our Conscious mind; and then the Conscious Mind feeds the Subconscious mind, which then forms the base of our habits.

To control what we experience in the world without, we must first gain control of the world within. We do this by canceling negative and destructive thoughts in our Conscious mind because they in turn become impressed on the Subconscious mind, which brings them into our reality through the Law of Attraction.

The exercise for this Week is of vital importance as we must learn to silence the internal dialogue that all of us have with ourselves every minute of every day, much of which leads to unintended and even unwanted results. By doing this exercise, we are doing two things: we are becoming conscious of the chatter that is occurring and we are disciplining ourselves to still that chatter.

As you progress, you will notice every time your mind begins its harsh and negative dialogue. When you notice that awful chatter, replace it with affirmations.

What Have We Learned?

I take charge of my life. I am responsible.

More Affirmations

I know where I am now. That is from where I start to build my life.

I know where I am going. I move toward my goals every day.

Every day and in every way, I am getting better and better.

I like myself. I deserve success. I am happy. I am healthy. I am wealthy.

Cause and effect is as absolute and undeviating in the hidden realm of thought as in the world of visible and material things. Mind is the master weaver, both of the interior garment of character and the outer garment of circumstance.

—James Allen

Week Three

Realizing Your Mental Resources

*The Letter of
Transmittal*

You have found that the Individual may act on the Universal, and that the result of this action and interaction is cause and effect.

Thought, therefore, is the cause and the experiences with which you meet in life are the effect.

Eliminate, therefore, any possible tendency to complain of conditions as they have been or as they are, because it rests with you to change them and make them what you would like them to be.

Direct your effort to a realization of the mental resources, always at your command, from which all real and lasting power comes.

Persist in this practice until you come to a realization of the fact that there can be no failure in the accomplishment of any proper object in life if you but understand your power and persist in your object, because the mind forces are ever ready to lend themselves to a purposeful will in the effort to crystallize thought and desire into actions, events, and conditions.

Whereas in the beginning each function of life and each action is the result of conscious thought, the habitual actions become automatic and the thought that controls them passes into the realm of the subconscious; yet it is just as intelligent as before. It is necessary that it become automatic, or subconscious, in order that the subconscious mind may attend to other things. The new actions will, however, in their turn, become habitual, then automatic, then subconscious in order that the mind again may be freed from this detail and advanced to still other activities.

When you realize this, you will have found a source of power which will enable you to take care of any situation in life which may develop.

The Main Points

The Cerebrospinal is the organ of the Conscious mind.

The Sympathetic is the organ of the Subconscious mind.

The Solar Plexus is the central point of distribution for the energy which the body is constantly generating.

The distribution of energy may be disrupted by resistant, critical, discordant thoughts; but especially by fear.

Every ill with which the human race is afflicted is the result of this disruption.

This energy may be controlled and directed by conscious thought.

Fear may be completely eliminated by an understanding and recognition of the true source of all power.

Our predominant mental attitude determines the experiences with which we meet in life.

To awaken the Solar Plexus, mentally concentrate upon the condition that we desire to see manifested in our lives.

The Universal Mind is the creative principle of the Universe.

The Exercise

For your exercise this week, I will ask you to go one step further. I want you to not only be perfectly still and inhibit all thought as far as possible, but relax. Let go. Let the muscles take their normal condition; this will remove all pressure from the nerves and eliminate that tension which so frequently produces physical exhaustion.

Your Life to the Max

Imagine that you are living life to the fullest. It is your dream, so dream big and lush and full. List the things you want most in life here. Do not limit yourself to this page! Get another sheet of paper (or even a legal pad) and write everything that you want, both big and small. Your list may contain things such as being debt-free to a $10 million mansion, from a new golf club to a Lear jet. Do not limit yourself, rather dream and list *everything* that you want.

1.

2.

3.

4.

5.

6.

7.

8.

9.

10.

11.

12.

13.

14.

15.

16.

17.

18.

19.

20.

We have found that the subconscious mind is responsive to our conscious will, which means that the unlimited creative power of the Universal Mind is within the control of the conscious mind of the individual.

Week Three

Relaxing the Body

While keeping the mind and the body still, you must now relax the body so as not to create any unwanted tension, which would disrupt the flow of energy through your body. As you have mastered the previous exercises, so you shall master this one.

As Haanel wrote, "Physical relaxation is a voluntary exercise of the will and the exercise will be found to be of great value, as it enables the blood to circulate freely to and from the brain and body."

By relaxing, we are allowing the Solar Plexus, which is the seat of the Unconscious Mind, to function completely. As we relax, we radiate confidence, health, and strength—all thing harmonious. As we relax, we experience nonresistant thought, which expands the Solar Plexus. By relaxing, we are conquering the personal devil, fear.

Fear is that which makes us agonize over the past, present, and future. When it is destroyed, our light will shine and we will be able to realize our full potential and we will be able to overcome any adverse condition.

Tension leads to mental unrest and abnormal mental activity, which produces worry, fear, and anxiety. Relaxation is therefore necessary to defeat this. When you master this exercise, your Solar Plexus will then be ready to function perfectly.

What do you think of this poem?

Week Three

My Wage

I bargained with Life for a penny,
And Life would pay no more,
However I begged at evening
When I counted my scanty store.

For Life is a just employer,
He gives you what you ask,
But once you have set the wages,
Why, you must bear the task.

I worked for a menial's hire,
Only to learn, dismayed,
That any wage I had asked of Life,
Life would have willingly paid.

—Jessie B. Rittenhouse

Week Four

Reversing the Process: Cause and Effect

**Week
Four**

*The Letter of
Transmittal*

Enclosed herewith I hand you Week Four. This part will show you why what you think, or do, or feel, is an indication of what you are.

Thought is energy, and energy is power, and it is because all the religions, sciences, and philosophies with which the world has heretofore been familiar have been based upon the manifestation of this energy instead of the energy itself, that the world has been limited to effects, while causes have been ignored or misunderstood.

For this reason we have God and the Devil in religion, positive and negative in science, and good and bad in philosophy.

The Master Key reverses the process; it is interested only in cause, and the letters received from students tell a marvelous story. They indicate conclusively that students are finding the cause whereby they may secure for themselves health, harmony, abundance, and whatever else may be necessary for their welfare and happiness.

Life is expressive and it is our business to express ourselves harmoniously and constructively. Sorrow, misery, unhappiness, disease, and poverty are not necessities and we are constantly eliminating them.

But this process of eliminating consists in rising above and beyond limitation of any kind. He who has strengthened and purified his thought need not concern himself about microbes, and he who has come into an understanding of the law of abundance will go at once to the source of supply.

It is thus that fate, fortune, and destiny will be controlled as readily as a captain controls his ship or an engineer his train.

The Main Points

Thought is spiritual energy.

Thought is carried by the law of vibration.

Thought is given vitality by the law of love.

Thought takes form by the law of growth.

The secret of the creative process is that it is a spiritual activity.

We may develop the faith, courage, and enthusiasm that will result in accomplishment by a recognition of our spiritual nature.

Service is the secret of Power.

Service is the secret of Power because we get what we give.

The Silence is a physical stillness.

The Silence is the first step to self-control and self-mastery.

The Exercise

Last week I asked you to relax, to let go physically. This week, I am going to ask you to let go mentally. If you practiced the exercise given you last week fifteen or twenty minutes a day in accordance with the instructions, you can no doubt relax physically; and anyone who cannot consciously do this quickly and completely is not a master of himself. He has not obtained freedom; he is still a slave to conditions. But I shall assume that you have mastered the exercise and are ready to take the next step, which is mental freedom.

This week, after taking your usual position, remove all tension by completely relaxing, then mentally let go of all adverse conditions, such as hatred, anger, worry, jealousy, envy, sorrow, trouble, or disappointment of any kind.

You may say that you cannot "let go" of these things, but you can. You can do so by mentally determining to do so by voluntary intention and persistence.

A Part of the Universal

The "I" of you is not your physical body, nor is it your mind. It is something that controls and directs the mind and the body. When you say "I think" the "I" tells the mind what to think; when you say "I go" the "I" tells the body where it shall go.

The "I" is spiritual and it is your connection to the Universal. It is a part of the Universal. The only difference between the "I" and the Universal is one of degree.

Week Four

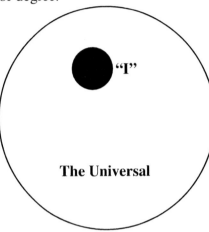

The world within is controlled by the "I" and this "I" is part of the Universal Energy or Spirit, which is usually called God.

Science calls the Universal the "Eternal Energy." Religion states that "God is dwelling *in* man rather than operating *on* men from without."

The Bible says, "Know ye not that ye are the temple of the living God?"

The Secret of Power

In order to be able to do things, we must have power. Being spiritual or attaining mastery does not mean to go without things or to become self-denying, as an ascetic. How can one help others if one is not sufficiently powerful? Only a person with wealth can donate to a charity; only a person with strength can defend the little man; only a person with knowledge can give advice to the unexperienced.

The way we get this power is to be of service. The more we give, the more we get. For example, suppose two people invested in a stock and the stock over time doubled in value. The first person invested $1,000, thus he increased his wealth to $2,000, a profit of $1,000. The second person invested $10,000. His wealth increased to $20,000 and he profited $10,000!

The same holds true for all aspects of life: relationships, learning, work, and play. If one wishes to learn mathematics, the person who does more exercises or practice problems (gives more) will be the one who learns more. The person who invests more of himself at work will be the person who is promoted more often. A musician cannot play at Carnegie Hall unless he "practices, practices, practices" (gives, gives, gives).

The only time this will fail is if we pursue selfish ends that hurt others or bring deficits to others. It is not wrong to profit, but it is wrong to profit unjustly by cheating or deceiving others. When you allow the Universal to work through you, then you will be able to attain all that you desire; when you are busy with your own selfish plans and schemes, you will fail.

In **Week Three**, you were to list everything that you wanted in life. Hopefully, it is a long and comprehensive list. It should contain both the big and the small.

*Get into Action—
Now!*

What you are to do here is peruse that want-list and list here the top ten things you can accomplish immediately. Let's say you wrote "I want Haanel's other book, *The Amazing Secrets of the Yogi*." Well, write that here.

1.

2.

3.

4.

5.

6.

7.

8.

9.

10.

Once you have your list of things that you can accomplish immediately, go and do those things! Life is about doing. You can have the greatest idea or dream in the world, but if you do nothing about it, then you are nothing but an idle dreamer and the best in you is wasted. Think of what made the successful people successful: *It was the fact that they did something!* Even the great thinkers became known as "great thinkers" because they took action—they wrote their ideas on paper for all to see.

*"I Can Be What I
Will To Be."*

There is a caveat, though. As Haanel says, "If you do not intend to do a thing, do not start. If you do start a thing, see it through even if the heavens fall; if you make up your mind to do something, do it; let nothing or no one interfere."

Every time we set ourselves to do something and we accomplish it, no matter how great or small, we are depositing currency in our spiritual checkbook. When we fail to accomplish something, we are withdrawing currency. If we withdraw too much, then we bankrupt ourselves. It is vitally important to see through what we intend to do.

A Key Point

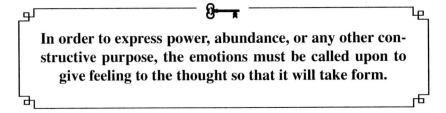

In order to express power, abundance, or any other constructive purpose, the emotions must be called upon to give feeling to the thought so that it will take form.

Seek the Silence

Thought is the secret to all attainment. This is because when we think, we set into motion the **law of vibration**, which carries our thoughts so that they can become reality. The **law of love**, which works through the emotions, gives these thoughts vitality.

Your level of belief will influence how quickly your dreams become reality. Look at it this way: When you believe that something is easily attainable, then you step quickly to attain that desire. On the other hand, when you believe that what you want is "out of your reach" or a "pipe dream", then you stall and stutter on your way, which either drastically slows your journey or impedes it completely.

We set our thoughts into motion by seeking the Silence. It is in the Silence that we can be still, and when we are still, we can think, and thought is the secret to all attainment.

As we think something more and more and see it clearer and clearer, it finally becomes automatic in our mind. We really know what we think. It moves from being a mere thought to a fact. **"We are sure; we know."**

Guided by the Intellect

For everything to work, we must be guided by the intellect rather than the emotions. For those of you familiar with E-mail, this example will strike home. E-mail is a wonderful way to communicate with someone instantly. When one sends an E-mail, the recipient receives the E-mail almost instantly, thus facilitating easy communication. If someone should receive an E-mail that makes them angry, though, it is very easy for the person to respond in a very emotional way, which may result in hurt feelings or worse. Common E-mail etiquette states that when one receives an E-mail that makes one angry, rather than replying with an emotional outburst, take a moment and *think* about what you are writing and what the consequences may be.

The key is that we must think. While the emotions propel our thoughts, they must be correct and true thoughts, rather than emotional or reflexive outbursts.

The will guided by the intellect will gain victory.

Week Four

The key of this exercise, like the exercise in **Week Three**, is to "let go." By letting go of the things that drag ourselves down, we shall attain the life that we desire. Some people refer to this as "dropping our baggage" or "laying down your cross."

Haanel states that if you are having trouble with letting go, you must mentally determine to do so by voluntary intention and persistence. That is one way. Here is a method that should help you with letting go.

If you find yourself unable to let go of certain feelings, then write down what that is. For example, if you are angry with someone for teasing you in high school, then write it down. When you have compiled your list, read it. I bet most (if not all) of those items look pretty silly. Look how little they look on paper! Realize how miniscule they are when compared to the grandness of your life.

Now you should be able to let those things go.

Week Four

Week
Four

"Plan ahead. It wasn't raining when Noah built the ark."

—Unknown

"The will is the strong blind man who carries on his shoulders
the lame man who can see."

—Arthur Schopenhauer

Week Five

The Creative Mind

***The Letter of
Transmittal***

Enclosed herewith you will find Week Five. After studying this part carefully, you will see that every conceivable force or object or fact is the result of mind in action.

Mind in action is thought, and thought is creative. Men are thinking now as they never thought before. Therefore, this is a creative age, and the world is awarding its richest prizes to the thinkers.

Matter is powerless, passive, inert. Mind is force, energy, power. Mind shapes and controls matter. Every form which matter takes is but the expression of some preexisting thought.

But thought works no magic transformations; it obeys natural laws; it sets in motion natural forces; it releases natural energies; it manifests in your conduct and actions, and these in turn react upon your friends and acquaintances, and eventually upon the whole of your environment.

You can originate thought and, since thoughts are creative, you can create for yourself the things you desire.

At least ninety percent (90%) of your mental life is subconscious.

This vast mental storehouse is not generally utilized because few understand or appreciate the fact that it is an activity that they may consciously direct.

The conscious mind received its governing tendencies from heredity, which means that it is the result of all the environments of all past generations.

The law of attraction is bringing to us our "own," which is what we inherently are and is the result of our past thinking, both conscious and subconscious.

The thoughts that we entertain is the material with which we construct our mental home.

The Secret of Power is a recognition of the omnipresence of omnipotence.

All life and all power originates within.

The possession of power is contingent upon a proper use of the power already in our possession.

Now, go to your room, take the same seat, the same position as heretofore, and mentally select a place which has pleasant associations. Make a complete mental picture of it—see the buildings, the grounds, the trees, friends, associations, everything complete. At first, you will find yourself thinking of everything under the sun, except the ideal upon which you desire to concentrate. But do not let that discourage you. Persistence will win, but persistence requires that you practice these exercises every day without fail.

"The Word Has Become Flesh"

❝The mind, which pervades the body, is largely the result of heredity, which, in turn, is simply the result of all the environments of all past generations on the responsive and ever moving life forces.❞

Heredity determines many of our basic characteristics and traits. On the surface level, we get most of our traits from our parents. These traits go beyond the physical, such as eye colour and hair colour; we are also imbued with tendencies toward other traits, such as political affiliation, smoking and drinking, the way we talk, and other sundry characteristics. These characteristics are passed to us by the fact that we are influenced by our parents (or primary care-givers) from birth, and even before birth as we receive vibrations and impressions when we are in the womb. All of these impressions are the foundation upon which our mental world is constructed.

These impressions continue throughout one's life. We are influenced by our home, business, and social environment, where we receive from others opinions, suggestions, and statements.

We are thus the result of our past thinking and we will become what we are thinking today. The Law of Attraction will bring to us "our own."

If a child is born to a family of alcoholics and as that child matures he sees his parents imbibing daily, then chances are good that he, too, will move from the baby bottle to the liquor bottle. It is similar in almost every aspect and permutation. A child of Republican parents will probably become a Republican; middle-class parents will raise a middle-class child; honest and integrous parents will beget honest children. Look around, the trend is true.

Why is this? If we see something enough, then we see that it is true. (Not good or bad, per se, because the subconscious does not judge. It just accumulates.) As it is in the subconscious, it is then passed to the Sympathetic System, from there it is built into our physical body.

One of the first words a child learns is "No." Is it any wonder that later in life, when he wants to do something, his first thought is "No!"? The word has become so inculcated that it becomes the first response to just about any idea or thought—whether it is true or not.

A Key Point

> **The great fact is that the source of all life and all power is from within. Persons, circumstances, and events may suggest need and opportunities, but the insight, strength, and power to answer these needs will be found within.**

Week Five

The goal of the exercise for this Week is to have the mind concentrate on positive thoughts. With all of the exercises, we are learning to control ourselves—both body and mind. As we have seen, it can be quite difficult to merely keep the body still. It is even more difficult to quell our thoughts. As we shall see when we practice this exercise, directing and centering our thoughts is the most difficult.

We will succeed, though. In this exercise, you are to mentally envision a pleasant place with buildings and friends and anything that would make you happy. For example, you may want to imagine a happy family gathering at your house. For this exercise to be successful, you must make the picture complete. You are to practice until you can see every detail, smell every aroma, hear every voice, and feel every touch.

To help you, write a paragraph or so of your pleasant, ideal scene. As you write it, you will help to commit it to memory and it will help to keep your mind from wandering as you practice the exercise.

My pleasant place is...

Week Five

**The Quotable
Haanel**

The merchant who does not keep his goods going out will soon have none coming in; the corporation that fails to give efficient service will soon lack customers; the attorney who fails to get results will soon lack clients; and so it goes everywhere. Power is contingent upon a proper use of the power already in our possession: what is true in every field of endeavour, every experience in life, is true of the power from which every other power known among men is begotten—spiritual power. Take away the spirit and what is left? Nothing.

"Relation and connection are not somewhere and some time, but everywhere and always."

—Emerson

Week Six

The Brain of Man

The Letter of Transmittal

It is my privilege to enclose Week Six. This part will give you an excellent understanding of the most wonderful piece of mechanism which has ever been created. A mechanism whereby you may create for yourself Health, Strength, Success, Prosperity, or any other condition which you desire. Necessities are demands, and demands create action, and actions bring about results. The process of evolution is constantly building our tomorrows out of our todays. Individual development, like Universal development, must be gradual with an ever increasing capacity and volume.

The knowledge that if we infringe upon the rights of others, we become moral thorns and find ourselves entangled at every turn of the road, should be an indication that success is contingent upon the highest moral idea, which is "The greatest good to the greatest number."

Aspiration, desire, and harmonious relations constantly and persistently maintained will accomplish results. The greatest hindrance is erroneous and fixed ideas.

To be in tune with eternal truth we must possess poise and harmony within. In order to receive intelligence the receiver must be in tune with the transmitter.

Thought is a product of Mind and Mind is creative, but this does not mean that the Universal will change its modus operandi to suit us or our ideas, but it does mean that we can come into harmonious relationship with the Universal, and when we have accomplished this we may ask anything to which we are entitled, and the way will be made plain.

Heat, light, power, and music are some of the effects that can be produced by electricity.

The Main Points

These effects depend upon the mechanism to which the electricity is attached.

The result of the action and interaction—of the individual mind upon the Universal—is the conditions and experiences with which we meet.

These conditions may be changed by changing the mechanism by which the Universal is differentiated in form.

This mechanism is the brain.

The brain may be changed by the process we call thinking. Thoughts produce brain cells, and these cells respond to the corresponding thought in the Universal.

The power of concentration is the very highest personal accomplishment that can be acquired. It is the distinguishing characteristic of every successful man or woman.

The power of concentration may be acquired by faithfully practicing the exercises outlined in this System.

It is important to acquire the power of concentration because it will enable us to control our thoughts, and since thoughts are causes, then conditions must be effects. If we can control the cause, then we can also control the effect.

Men learning the basic methods of constructive thinking is changing conditions and multiplying results in the objective world.

In order to cultivate the power of attention, bring a photograph with you to the same seat in the same room in the same position as heretofore. Examine it closely at least ten minutes: Note the expression of the eyes, the form of the features, the clothing, the way the hair is arranged—in fact, note every detail shown on the photograph carefully. Now cover it and close your eyes and try to see it mentally. If you can see every detail perfectly and can form a good mental image of the photograph, you are to be congratulated; if not repeat the process until you can.

The Exercise

This step is simply for the purpose of preparing the soil; next week we shall be ready to sow the seed.

It is by such exercises as these that you will finally be able to control your mental moods, your attitude, your consciousness.

Man's mind stretched to a new idea never goes back to its original dimensions.

—Oliver Wendell Holmes

Week
Six

Man has accomplished the seemingly impossible because he has refused to consider it impossible. By concentration, men have made the connection between the finite and the Infinite, the limited and the Unlimited, the visible and the Invisible, the personal and the Impersonal.

—Charles F. Haanel, *Master Key Arcana*

The nervous system is an electrical system. It is powered by the mind and the currents course through the spinal cord and through the nerves. Every thought sets the brain cells into action. If the thought is sufficiently refined and concentrated, then the thought expresses itself perfectly.

Your Mental Dynamo

The key to attaining what we want, then, is to develop the mental dynamo so that it has laser-like focus and power. **We must develop and exercise our power of concentration.**

Focus and concentration are the most distinguishing factors of highly successful men and women. It is not often that the smartest man achieves great heights. As Calvin Coolidge stated:

> Nothing in the world can take the place of Persistence. Talent will not; nothing is more common than unsuccessful men with talent. Genius will not; unrewarded genius is almost a proverb. Education will not; the world is full of educated derelicts. Persistence and determination alone are omnipotent. The slogan 'Press On' has solved and always will solve the problems of the human race.

Larry Ellison, the billionaire CEO of Oracle, said about Bill Gates, "Bill Gates wants people to think he's Edison, when he's really Rockefeller. Referring to Gates as the smartest man in America isn't right…wealth isn't the same thing as intelligence." One thing everyone will say about Mr. Gates, though, is the fact that he is driven and has a laser-like focus when he sets to do something.

Think of it this way: if you take a magnifying glass and focus the rays of the sun, then you can start a fire. When the sunlight is scattered, nothing will happen. Focus those rays and watch out! The same goes for the mind. If you allow power to be dissipated by jumping from one thought to the next, no result will be apparent; but if you focus and concentrate on a single purpose for a length of time, then nothing is impossible.

A Key Point

> **Growth follows knowledge; action follows inspiration; opportunity follows perception. Always the spiritual first, then the transformation into the infinite and illimitable possibilities of achievement.**

Practicing the Exercise

All of the exercises contained in *The Master Key System* are geared toward strengthening the source of our thought and power—the mind. They should be practiced diligently and to the point of perfection.

This exercise is key to strengthening our powers of concentration and also recollection. As we improve this, we enable ourselves to become more receptive to the thoughts and ideas that bombard us each and every day.

Why is it, though, that a youth has no problem memorizing the lyrics to his or her favourite song, yet they can remember a poem or historical passage only with great difficulty?

The answer lies with what we have learned earlier: relaxation. When the youth is listening to music that he enjoys, his body and mind are relaxed, thus making him receptive to the input he receives. When he is asked to memorize a poem or something of similar nature, his tension rises, making his mind hard to penetrate and then only with great effort.

We should have learned by now to relax the body and mind and to let things flow from the Universal. Thus, when doing this exercise, relax.

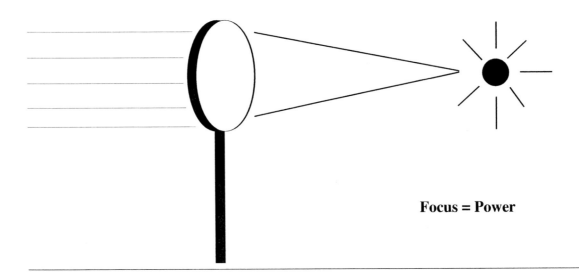

Focus = Power

Week Seven

Utilizing the Omnipotent Power

The Letter of Transmittal

Through all the ages man has believed in an invisible power, through which and by which all things have been created and are continually being re-created.

We may personalize this power and call it God, or we may think of it as the essence, or spirit, which permeates all things, but in either case the effect is the same.

So far as the individual is concerned, the objective, the physical, the visible, is the personal—that which can be cognized by the senses. It consists of body, brain, and nerves. The subjective is the spiritual, the invisible, the impersonal.

The personal is conscious because it is a personal entity. The impersonal, being the same in kind and quality as all other Being, is not conscious of itself and has therefore been termed the subconscious.

The personal, or conscious, has the power of will and choice, and can therefore exercise discrimination in the selection of methods whereby to bring about the solution of difficulties.

The impersonal, or spiritual, being a part or one with the source and origin of all power, can necessarily exercise no such choice, but, on the contrary, it has Infinite resources at its command. It can and does bring about results by methods concerning which the human or individual mind can have no possible conception.

You will therefore see that it is your privilege to depend upon the human will with all its limitations and misconceptions, or you may utilize the potentialities of Infinity by making use of the subconscious mind. Here, then, is the scientific explanation of the wonderful power which has been put within your control, if you but understand, appreciate, and recognize it.

One method of consciously utilizing this omnipotent power is outlined in Week Seven, which I have the honor of transmitting herewith.

Week Seven

Visualization is the process of making mental pictures.   *The Main Points*

The result of this method of thought is that by holding the image or picture in mind, we can gradually but surely bring the thing nearer to us. We can be what we will to be.

Idealization is a process of visualizing or idealizing the plans that will eventually materialize in our objective world.

Clearness and accuracy are necessary because "seeing" creates "feeling" and "feeling" creates "being." First the mental, then the emotional, then the illimitable possibilities of achievement.

Each repeated action renders the image more accurate than the former one.

The material for the construction of your mental image is secured by millions of mental workers called brain cells.

The necessary conditions for bringing about the materialization of your ideal in the objective world is secured by the Law of Attraction, the natural law by which all conditions and experiences are brought about.

The three steps necessary to bring this law into operation are (1) Earnest Desire; (2) Confident Expectation; and (3) Firm Demand.

Many fail because they concentrate on loss, disease, and disaster. The law is operating perfectly; the things they fear are coming upon them.

The alternative is to concentrate on the ideals taht you desire to see manifested in your life.

Week
Seven

For your exercise this week, visualize your friend. See him exactly as you   *The Exercise*
last saw him. See the room, the furniture, recall the conversation. Now see his face, see it distinctly. Now talk to him about some subject of mutual interest; see his expression change, watch him smile. Can you do this? All right, you can; then arouse his interest, tell him a story of adventure, see his eyes light up with the spirit of fun or excitement. Can you do all of this? If so, your imagination is good, you are making excellent progress.

Think BIG

In his book, *The Art of the Deal*, Donald Trump writes this:

> I like thinking big. I always have. To me it's very simple: if you're going to be thinking anyway, you might as well think big. Most people think small, because most people are afraid of success, afraid of making decisions, afraid of winning. And that gives people like me a great advantage…One of the keys to thinking big is total focus. I think of it almost as a controlled neurosis, which is a quality I've noticed in many highly successful entrepreneurs. They're obsessive, they're driven, they're single-minded and sometimes they're almost maniacal, but it's all channeled into their work.

Make Your Ideal Real

A mental image is the mold from which your future will emerge. Visualization is the process by which you create these mental images. As you make your image clear and detailed and accurate, you will gradually bring the thing nearer to you until you eventually have it.

The three steps of visualization are:

1. Idealization
Picture in your mind what you want exactly as you want it. A mason will not lay a single brick without a blueprint nor will a writer begin a book without a detailed outline in mind. Before you plant a seed, you want to know what the harvest is to be.

2. Visualization
You must see the picture more and more complete. Thought will lead to action, action will develop methods, methods will develop friends, and friends will bring about circumstances.

3. Materialization
You will have what you desired.

A Key Point

The law is that thought will manifest in form, and only one who knows how to be the divine thinker of his own thoughts can ever take a Master's place and speak with authority.

As has become obvious, the exercises presented by Haanel are to strengthen the mind so as to be a dynamo for visualizing that which we desire while at the same time repressing the things that we do not desire.

In order to visualize, you will be using mental muscles that you may have never used before this time, or the muscles may have been used incorrectly or only in a limited capacity. Some people find visualization easy, while others have some difficulty with it. In general, left-handed people tend to have an easier time visualizing. Why is that? It is because of the different parts of the brain that are being put to use on a daily basis.

Those who are left-handed use the right side of their brain more. The right side of the brain is the seat of creativity and mental pictures and feelings. Those who are right-handed use the left side of their brain more. The left side of the brain is the seat of logic and deduction and language.

To help you visualize your friend as you are asked to do in this Week's exercise, write a description of him here, but use your opposite hand to write it. In other words, if you are right-handed (as most people are), then write with your left hand. If you are left-handed, then write the description with your right hand. This will serve to jump start the side of the brain that we do not exercise enough. It would be the ultimate goal to become ambidextrous, but that is not necessary. If you can, though, write with your opposite hand a couple of times per month so that you attain a decent level of competance at writing with that hand.

My friend is... (written with the opposite hand!)

Be ready to act when the time comes.

—Charles F. Haanel, *The Master Key System*

Week
Seven

Week Eight

Thought and Its Results

**The Letter of
Transmittal**

Week Eight is enclosed herewith. In this Part you will find that you may freely choose what you think, but the result of your thought is governed by all immutable law! Is not this a wonderful thought? Is it not wonderful to know that our lives are not subject to caprice or variability of any kind? That they are governed by law. This stability is our opportunity, because by complying with the law we can secure the desired effect with invariable precision.

It is the Law which makes the Universe one grand paean of Harmony. If it were not for law, the Universe would be a Chaos instead of a Cosmos.

Here, then, is the secret of the origin of both good and evil; this is all the good and evil there ever was or ever will be.

Let me illustrate. Thought results in action. If your thought is constructive and harmonious, the result will be good; if your thought is destructive or inharmonious, the result will be evil.

There is therefore but one law, one principle, one cause, one Source of Power, and good and evil are simply words which have been coined to indicate the result of our action, or our compliance or noncompliance with this law.

The importance of this is well illustrated in the lives of Emerson and Carlyle. Emerson loved the good and his life was a symphony of peace and harmony. Carlyle hated the bad, and his life was a record of perpetual discord and inharmony.

Here we have two grand men, each intent upon achieving the same ideal, but one makes use of constructive thought and is therefore in harmony with Natural Law, the other makes use of destructive thought and therefore brings upon himself discord of every kind and character.

It is evident therefore that we are to hate nothing—not even the "bad"—because hatred is destructive, and we shall soon find that by entertaining destructive thought we are sowing the "wind" and shall reap the "whirlwind."

The imagination is a form of constructive thought. It is the light by which we penetrate new worlds of thought and experience—the mighty instrument by which every inventor or discoverer opened the way from precedent to experience.

The cultivation of the imagination leads to the development of the ideal out of which your future will emerge.

The imagination may be cultivated by exercise. It must be supplied with nourishment or it cannot live.

Day dreaming is a form of mental dissipation, while imagination is a form of constructive thought that must precede every constructive action.

Mistakes are the result of ignorance.

Knowledge is the result of man's ability to think.

Mind is the ever moving force with which successful men secure the persons and circumstances necessary to complete their plans.

The ideal held steadily in mind attracts the necessary conditions for its fulfillment.

Keen analytical observation leads to the development of imagination, insight, perception, and sagacity.

Those traits lead to opulence and harmony.

The Exercise

Last week you created a mental image—you brought it from the invisible into the visible. This week I want you to take an object and follow it back to its origination, see of what it really consists. If you do this you will develop imagination, insight, perception, and sagacity. These come not by the superficial observation of the multitude, but by a keen analytical observation which sees below the surface.

Take the same position as heretofore and visualize a Battleship. See the grim monster floating on the surface of the water; there appears to be no life anywhere about; all is silence; you know that by far the largest part of the vessel is under water; out of sight; you know that the ship is as large and as heavy as a twenty-story skyscraper; you know that there are hundreds of men ready to spring to their appointed task instantly; you know that every department is in charge of able, trained, skilled officials who have proven themselves competent to take charge of this marvelous piece of mechanism; you know that although it lies apparently oblivious to everything else, it has eyes which see everything for miles around, and nothing is permitted to

Continued on next page...

*The Exercise
Continued*

escape its watchful vision; you know that while it appears quiet, submissive and innocent, it is prepared to hurl a steel projectile weighing thousands of pounds at an enemy many miles away; this and much more you can bring to mind with comparatively no effort whatever. But how did the battleship come to be where it is; how did it come into existence in the first place? All of this you want to know if you are a careful observer.

Follow the great steel plates through the foundries and see the thousands of men employed in their production. Go still further back and see the ore as it comes from the mine, see it loaded on barges or cars, see it melted and properly treated. Go back still further and see the architect and engineers who planned the vessel; let the thought carry you back still further in order to determine why they planned the vessel; you will see that you are now so far back that the vessel is something intangible, it no longer exists, it is now only a thought existing in the brain of the architect; but from where did the order come to plan the vessel? Probably from the Secretary of War; but probably this vessel was planned long before the war was thought of, and that Congress had to pass a bill appropriating the money; possibly there was opposition, and speeches for or against the bill. Whom do these Congressmen represent? They represent you and me, so that our line of thought begins with the Battleship and ends with ourselves, and we find in the last analysis that our own thought is responsible for this and many other things, of which we seldom think, and a little further reflection will develop the most important fact of all and that is, if someone had not discovered the law by which this tremendous mass of steel and iron could be made to float upon the water, instead of immediately going to the bottom, the battleship could not have come into existence at all.

This law is that, "the specific gravity of any substance is the weight of any volume of it, compared with an equal volume of water." The discovery of this law revolutionized every kind of ocean travel, commerce, and warfare, and made the existence of the battleship possible.

You will find exercises of this kind invaluable. When the thought has been trained to look below the surface everything takes on a different appearance, the insignificant becomes significant, the uninteresting interesting; the things which we supposed to be of no importance are seen to be the only really vital things in existence.

A Key Point

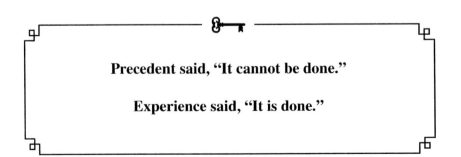

Precedent said, "It cannot be done."

Experience said, "It is done."

Imagine that you have died. You lived the life that you wanted. It was full and lush and replete with success and all of your earthly desires. An obituary was written about you. What does it say?

Write that article the way you would like to see it written. Leave nothing out. Talk about your character, your accomplishments, your family life, your experiences, everything as you would like to see it written by a newspaper reporter. You can make it as long as you want. If you need extra paper, then add as many pages as you need. This may very well be one of the most important exercises you will ever do.

The Life And Times Of _____

**Just Like
Sherlock Holmes**

In the famous tales by Sir Arthur Conan Doyle, the master sleuth, Sherlock Holmes, used a method of solving crimes called **deduction**. Basically, deduction is when one begins with a result and takes steps backwards in order to discover how the result came to be. It requires knowledge, logic, and, above all, a good imagination. By studying *The Master Key System*, you are building these traits within yourself, thus you have them handy.

From the obituary that you've written, take each event or goal and deduce how you would have accomplished it. What knowledge would you need? How many people would it take? How much money will it cost? For example, if you wrote that you became CEO of IBM, you may deduce that you applied for a job there until you were hired; from there you worked and produced more than was expected of you because you were working with things that interested you; you attended school to study the things you would need to know to get promoted; and so on until you finally attained your goal.

If you do not know what you will need, then do some research! Use libraries, book stores, and the Internet. Make contact with people who can answer your questions. Observe. After all, it's all elementary.

What I Need To Achieve

I.

    1.
    2.
    3.
    4.
    5.

II.

    1.
    2.
    3.
    4.
    5.

III.

    1.
    2.
    3.
    4.
    5.

Week Nine

Affirmations and Your Mind

The Letter of Transmittal

Week Nine is enclosed herewith. In this part you may learn to fashion the tools by which you may build for yourself any condition you desire.

If you wish to change conditions you must change yourself. Your whims, your wishes, your fancies, your ambitions may be thwarted at every step, but your inmost thoughts will find expression just as certainly as the plant springs from the seed.

Suppose, then, we desire to change conditions. How are we to bring this about? The reply is simple: By the law of growth. Cause and effect are as absolute and undeviating in the hidden realm of thought as in the world of material things.

Hold in mind the condition desired; affirm it as an already existing fact. This indicates the value of a powerful affirmation. By constant repetition it becomes a part of ourselves. We are actually changing ourselves; we are making ourselves what we want to be.

Character is not a thing of chance, but it is the result of continued effort. If you are timid, vacillating, self-conscious, or if you are over-anxious or harassed by thoughts of fear or impending danger, remember that it is axiomatic that "two things cannot exist in the same place at the same time." Exactly the same thing is true in the mental and spiritual world; so that your remedy is plainly to substitute thoughts of courage, power, self-reliance, and confidence, for those of fear, lack, and limitation.

The easiest and most natural way to do this is to select an affirmation which seems to fit your particular case. The positive thought will destroy the negative as certainly as light destroys darkness, and the results will be just as effectual.

Action is the blossom of thought, and conditions are the result of action so that you constantly have in your possession the tools by which you will certainly and inevitably make or unmake yourself, and joy or suffering will

Well-doing is the imperative condition of all well-being.

The Main Points

Right thinking is the condition precedent to every right action.

To know the Truth is the underlying condition necessary in every business transaction or social relation.

The result of a knowledge of the Truth is that we can readily foretell the result of any action that is based upon a true premise.

We can form no conception of the results that may ensue when action is based upon a false premise.

We may know the Truth by a realization of the fact that Truth is the vital principle of the Universe and is therefore omnipresent.

The nature of Truth is spiritual.

The secret of the solution to every problem is to apply spiritual Truth.

The advantage of spiritual methods is that they are always available.

A recognition of the omnipotence of spiritual power and a desire to become the recipient of its beneficent effects are the necessary requirements to use spiritual methods.

This week visualize a plant. Take a flower, the one you most admire, and bring it from the unseen into the seen. Plant the tiny seed, water it, care for it, place it where it will get the direct rays of the morning sun. See the seed burst; it is now a living thing, something which is alive and beginning to search for the means of subsistence. See the roots penetrating the earth, watch them shoot out in all directions and remember that they are living cells dividing and subdividing and that they will soon number millions, that each cell is intelligent, that it knows what it wants and knows how to get it. See the stem shoot forward and upward, watch it burst through the surface of the earth, see it divide and form branches, see how perfect and symmetrical each branch is formed, see the leaves begin to form, and then the tiny stems, each one holding aloft a bud, and as you watch you see the bud begin to unfold and your favorite flower comes to view; and now if you will concentrate intently you will become conscious of a fragrance. It is the fragrance of the flower as the breeze gently sways the beautiful creation which you have visualized.

The Exercise

When you are enabled to make your vision clear and complete you will be enabled to enter into the spirit of a thing; it will become very real to you; you will be learning to concentrate and the process is the same, whether you are concentrating on health, a favorite flower, an ideal, a complicated business proposition, or any other problem of life.

Week Nine

It's Good to be Me

Make a list of everything you like about yourself. It could be anything, such as you're a smart dresser or you have great friends or you know how to play the piano. List them now.

1.

2.

3.

4.

5.

6.

7.

8.

9.

10.

If you need more room, then get another piece of paper and keep going!

When It's Time to Change...

In this space, make a list of things you would like to change about yourself, such as you tend to procrastinate or you eat too many sweets or you have trouble with math. Write your list now.

1.

2.

3.

4.

5.

6.

7.

8.

9.

Week Nine

Now you are going to take the list of things that you would like to change about yourself and write an affirmation that will help you to change it. For example, if you want to stop smoking, then you would write "I am smoke-free." If you wish to become less shy, then you will write "I am outgoing and friendly."

From a Negative to a Positive

Remember, when writing an affirmation, write it using the present tense. Also write it so it is stated as a positive statement. For example, we do not use as an affirmation "I will not smoke." We write "I am smoke-free." Instead of writing "I am not in debt," write "I have a positive cash flow" or "I am wealthy."

My List of Affirmations

1.

2.

3.

4.

5.

6.

7.

8.

9.

10.

A Key Point

He who has learned to bring the greatest spiritual truths into touch with the so-called lesser things of life has discovered the secret of the solution of his problem.

Week Nine

Is the Record Skipping?

To some, the exercises may seem a little bit repetitive. Why must I write affirmations again? Make another list of goals? Again?

There is a reason for all of this. Notice that all of the exercises are subtly different. They may be similar, but there are small changes. While the changes may be miniscule at times, they are significant enough that they produce a somewhat different list.

The main reason, though, is that you can never write your goals or affirmations enough. There is one thing that all high-achievers and attainers have in common.

All successful people write their goals!

A study of the population showed that 83% of the population do not have clearly defined goals; 14% have goals, but they are not written; and 3% of the population has written goals.

Here's the kicker: *The 3% that have written goals earn ten times as much as the 83% group.* The 3-percenters also tend to be healthier and have happier marriages. The moral of the story is write your goals and refer to them often!

In this space, rewrite your goals. Remember to write them in the present tense and in the form of a positive statement. For example, "My income is $10,000 per month." "I am healthy and strong." "I am the district manager for my company."

My Goals

1.

2.

3.

4.

5.

6.

7.

8.

**Refer to your goals every day and repeat them as you do
your affirmations.**

Week Ten

A Certain Definite Cause

The Letter of Transmittal

If you get a thorough understanding of the thought contained in Week Ten, you will have learned that nothing happens without a definite cause. You will be enabled to formulate your plans in accordance with exact knowledge. You will know how to control any situation by bringing adequate causes into play. When you win, as you will, you will know exactly why.

The ordinary man, who has no definite knowledge of cause and effect, is governed by his feeling or emotions. He thinks chiefly to justify his action. If he fails as a business man, he says that luck is against him. If he dislikes music, he says that music is an expensive luxury. If he is a poor office man, he says that he could succeed better at some outdoor work. If he lacks friends, he says his individuality is too fine to be appreciated.

He never thinks his problem through to the end. In short, he does not know that every effect is the result of a certain definite cause, but he seeks to console himself with explanations and excuses. He thinks only in self-defense.

On the contrary, the man who understands that there is no effect without an adequate cause thinks impersonally. He gets down to bed rock facts regardless of consequences. He is free to follow the trail of truth wherever it may lead. He sees the issue clear to the end and he meets the requirements fully and fairly, and the result is that the world gives him all that it has to give in friendship, honor, love, and approval.

The Main Points

Wealth is the offspring of power.

Possessions are of value only as they confer power.

A knowledge of cause and effect enables men to plan courageously and execute fearlessly.

Life originates in the inorganic world only by the introduction of some living form. There is no other way.

Thought is the connecting link between the finite and the Infinite because the Universal can manifest only through the individual.

Causation depends upon polarity. A circuit must be formed. The Universal is the positive side of the battery of life, the individual is the negative, and thought forms the circuit.

Many fail to secure harmonious conditions because they do not understand the law. There is no polarity and they have not formed the circuit.

The remedy is a conscious recognition of the law of attraction with the intention of bringing it into existence for a definite purpose.

The result is that thought will correlate with its object and bring it into manifestation, because thought is a product of the spiritual man and spirit is the Creative Principle of the Universe.

The Exercise

This week select a blank space on the wall, or any other convenient spot, from where you usually sit. Mentally draw a black horizontal line about six inches long, try to see the line as plainly as though it were painted on the wall. Now mentally draw two vertical lines connecting with this horizontal line at either end. Now draw another horizontal line connecting with the two vertical lines. Now you have a square. Try to see the square perfectly. When you can do so, draw a circle within the square. Now place a point in the center of the circle. Now draw the point toward you about 10 inches. Now you have a cone on a square base. You will remember that your work was all in black. Change it to white, to red, to yellow.

If you can do this, you are making excellent progress and will soon be enabled to concentrate on any problem you may have in mind.

"Know Thyself"

The great philosopher, Socrates, learned from the oracle at Delphi the motto, "Know thyself." It means that instead of relying merely on outward appearances, one should know himself in order to know the true good.

MiMi Paris in her book, *Size Matters!*, says the same thing. She says that we continually lie to ourselves about things so as to remove the responsibility of our actions from our shoulders. Rather than look into the mirror and see the truth, we would rather lie and feel "good" about ourselves. Rather than see a deficiency as an opportunity for improvement, we use a deficiency as a crutch or an appeal to someone's pity.

We are all a part of the Universal and that Universal is able to express itself through us if we allow it. We must act in accordance with its laws. When we do, the gates will be let open and we will be able to partake in all of its abundance.

A Key Point

> **Abundance is a natural law of the Universe. The evidence of this law is conclusive; we see it on every hand. Everywhere Nature is lavish, wasteful, extravagant. Nowhere is economy observed in any created thing.**

The Circuit

In order to act in accordance with the laws, one must use the tools that we have properly. We must complete the circuit. The Universal is connected to the individual by thought. As we think thoughts of power, wealth, and harmony, we charge ourselves and that attracts to us the things we want.

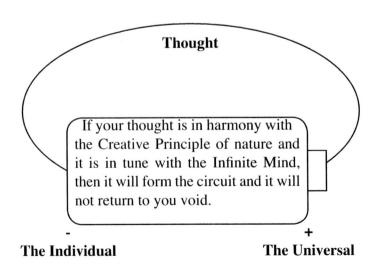

Thought

If your thought is in harmony with the Creative Principle of nature and it is in tune with the Infinite Mind, then it will form the circuit and it will not return to you void.

-   **+**
The Individual   **The Universal**

Think of a time in your life when you were 100% successful, when there was something that you did—a task, event, or challenge—that you completed and when it was done, you knew that it was perfect. Remember the time, the place, people that were there. Remember whether it was daytime or night, what time of year, how you felt, everything you had to do or the things that you did. Write a few paragraphs about that time.

You Already Have
It Within You

Come to an understanding of what you did that resulted in your success. How did you feel? What emotions played a role? What knowledge did you have to use? Did you work hard or work smart? Write the "keys" to your success here.

Remember, you did it. When we come to an understanding that our power, our happiness, joy, and prosperity come from within, we may effortlessly recreate success in every area of our life.

Week Ten

A Tiger in a Cage

A teacher asked his student, "What holds a tiger within a cage?"

The student pondered the question for a moment and replied, " Teacher, it is the bars that holds a tiger within a cage."

The teacher shook his head and asked again, "What holds a tiger within a cage?"

Again the student pondered the question and again the student answered, " Surely, Teacher, it must be the bars that hold the tiger within the cage."

The teacher looked at the student, shook his head, and replied in a low voice, "My student, it is not the bars that hold the tiger within a cage, but the space between the bars that holds the tiger within a cage."

We have been taught that we are in a cage. We have been lead to believe that we cannot do things that we most certainly can.

Our thoughts are the bars of the cage, but it is our attitude that actually confines us.

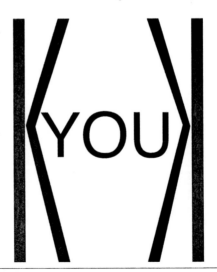

Week Eleven

Inductive Reasoning and the Objective Mind

The Letter of Transmittal

Your life is governed by law—by actual, immutable principles that never vary. Law is in operation at all times in all places. Fixed laws underlie all human actions. For this reason, men who control giant industries are enabled to determine with absolute precision just what percentage of every hundred thousand people will respond to any given set of conditions.

It is well, however, to remember that while every effect is the result of a cause, the effect in turn becomes a cause, which creates other effects, which in turn create still other causes; so that when you put the law of attraction into operation you must remember that you are starting a train of causation for good or otherwise which may have endless possibilities.

We frequently hear it said, "A very distressing situation came into my life, which could not have been the result of my thought, as I certainly never entertained any thought which could have such a result." We fail to remember that like attracts like in the mental world, and that the thought which we entertain brings to us certain friendships—companionships of a particular kind—and these in turn bring about conditions and environment, which in turn are responsible for the conditions of which we complain.

Inductive reasoning is the process of the objective mind by which we compare a number of separate instances with each other until we see the common factor that gives rise to all of them.

Inductive reasoning has resulted in the discovery of a reign of law that has marked an epoch in human progress.

Need, want, and desire induce, guide, and determine action.

The unerring solution to every problem is to believe that our desire has already been fulfilled. Its accomplishment will then follow.

Jesus, Plato, and Swedenborg advocated that method.

The result of the operation of that thought process is that we are thinking on the plane of the absolute and planting a seed, which if left undisturbed will germinate into fruition.

It is scientifically exact because it is Natural Law.

"Faith is the substance of things hoped for, the evidence of things unseen."

The Law of Attraction is the Law by which Faith is brought into manifestation.

The Law of Attraction has eliminated the elements of uncertainty and caprice from men's' lives and substituted law, reason, and certitude.

The Main Points

For your exercise this week, concentrate on the quotation taken from the Bible, "Whatsoever things ye desire, when ye pray, believe that ye receive them and ye shall have them." Notice that there is no limitation. "Whatsoever things" is very definite and implies that the only limitation which is placed upon us is in our ability to think, to be equal to the occasion, to rise to the emergency, to remember that Faith is not a shadow, but a substance, "the substance of things hoped for, the evidence of things not seen."

The Exercise

Shooting for the Moon

When President Kennedy decided in 1960 that the United States would put a man on the moon in ten years, most of the technology to accomplish the task was not yet available. The decision to set the goal—the belief in its possibility and the belief that it could be achieved—produced the necessary scientific and technological breakthroughs to make it possible, and the resulting spin-offs of these new technologies altered our lives for the better.

A Key Point

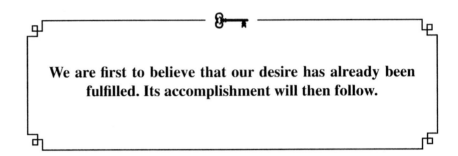

We are first to believe that our desire has already been fulfilled. Its accomplishment will then follow.

Those Goals Again

The Subconscious does not take into consideration time and space. It can only comprehend **Now**. Once we identify our goals, it is then necessary to affirm and visualize them in the **Here and Now**, as if they have already been completed.

What is a goal?
Personal instructions for a predetermined end-result.

Why have goals?
Definite plans produce definite results. Indefinite thinking typically produces no results. Be a 3-Percenter!

Why have goals in writing?
Unless written, objectives can become lost in the shuffle and excitement of daily activities and responsibilities. What may be crystal clear today, may become vague in the rush and urgency of tomorrow's affairs. Without written goals, memories may become hazy; motivation and purpose may become lost. Written goals serve as a reference or reminder of your needs, wants, and desires. Having a written goal, you know where you are going. You tend to gain from life the exact rewards you expect to achieve and receive.

Goals are intended to support your purpose, allowing you to always have everything in life you sincerely need, want, and desire.

In this section, you are going to make sort of a "life plan." You are going to list some of your immediate goals, goals for the near future, and your long-term goals. You may see some overlap with them, but that is OK. If you have a focused vision, then that is natural; if your vision is not yet focused, then this will help you to get it clear. As stated, remember to write your goals in the present tense, as if you already had them.

Goals, Goals, Goals

My Goals for This Month

1.
2.
3.
4.
5.

My Goals for This Year

1.
2.
3.
4.
5.

My Goals for The Next Five Years

1.
2.
3.
4.
5.

My Life Goals

1.
2.
3.
4.
5.

If you have more goals, then get more paper! When you have your goals, rewrite them on 3x5 cards and read them everyday.

Finish each day and be done with it. You have done what you could; some blunders and absurdities have crept in; forget them as soon as you can. Tomorrow is a new day; you shall begin it serenely and with too high a spirit to be encumbered with your old nonsense.

Treat a man as he is, and he will remain as he is. Treat a man as he could be, and he will become what he should be.

People only see what they are prepared to see.

The creation of a thousand forests is in one acorn.

Do the thing we fear, and death of fear is certain.

A man is usually more careful of his money than he is of his principles.

Week Twelve

The Power of Concentration

The Letter of Transmittal

Week Twelve is enclosed herewith. In the fourth paragraph you will find the following statement: "You must first have the knowledge of your power; second, the courage to dare; third, the faith to do."

If you concentrate upon the thoughts given, if you give them your entire attention, you will find a world of meaning in each sentence and will attract to yourself other thoughts in harmony with them, and you will soon grasp the full significance of the vital knowledge upon which you are concentrating.

Knowledge does not apply itself; we as individuals must make the application, and the application consists in fertilizing the thought with a living purpose.

The time and thought which most persons waste in aimless effort would accomplish wonders if properly directed with some special object in view. In order to do this, it is necessary to center your mental force upon a specific thought and hold it there to the exclusion of all other thoughts. If you have ever looked through the focusing screen of a camera, you found that when the object was not in focus, the impression was indistinct and possibly blurred; but when the proper focus was obtained the picture was clear and distinct. This illustrates the power of concentration. Unless you can concentrate upon the object which you have in view, you will have but a hazy, indifferent, vague, indistinct, and blurred outline of your ideal and the results will be in accordance with your mental picture.

Any purpose in life may best be accomplished through a scientific understanding of the spiritual nature of thought.

The Main Points

The three steps that are essential are: (1) The knowledge of our power; (2) the courage to dare; and (3) the faith to do.

The practical working knowledge is secured by an understanding of Natural laws.

The reward for understanding these laws is a conscious realization of our ability to adjust ourselves to Divine and unchanging principle.

The degree in which we realize that we cannot change the Infinite but must cooperate with it will indicate the degree of success with which we meet.

The principle which gives thought its dynamic power is the Law of Attraction, which rests on vibration, which in turn rests upon the Law of Love. Thought impregnated with love becomes invincible.

This law is irresistible because it is a Natural law. All Natural laws are irresistible and unchangeable and act with mathematical exactitude. There is no deviation or variation.

It sometimes seems difficult to find the solution to our problems in life for the same reason that it is sometimes difficult to find the correct solution to a difficult mathematical problem: The operator is uninformed or inexperienced.

It is impossible for the mind to grasp an entirely new idea because we have no corresponding vibratory brain cell capable of receiving the idea.

Wisdom is secured by concentration. It is an unfoldment. It comes from within.

This week go to the same room, take the same chair, and the same position as heretofore. Be sure to relax. Let go, both mentally and physically; always do this; never try to do any mental work under pressure; see that there are no tense muscles or nerves, that you are entirely comfortable. Now realize your unity with omnipotence; get into touch with this power, come into a deep and vital understanding, appreciation, and realization of the fact that your ability to think is your ability to act upon the Universal Mind and bring it into manifestation. Realize that it will meet any and every requirement; that you have exactly the same potential ability which any individual ever did have or ever will have, because each is but an expression or manifestation of the One. All are parts of the whole. There is no difference in kind or quality—the only difference being one of degree.

The Exercise

A Key Point

> **Things are created in the mental or spiritual world before they appear in the outward act or event. By the simple process of governing our thought forces today, we help create the events that will come into our lives in the future, perhaps even tomorrow.**

Nothing to Write This Week

This week, you are going to have some fun—and make some money! You are going to put into action what you have been learning. By the end of this exercise, you may be a few dollars wealthier than when you started. Sound good? Good.

Visualize a quarter in your mind, just as you have been taught to visualize. Imagine it vividly and in detail. Keep it ingrained in your mind. Take as long as you want to visualize that quarter, perhaps fifteen minutes or so.

Next, vividly visualize that you are going to find that quarter on the street. Imagine the scene of you taking a walk and finding a quarter somewhere, perhaps when you are walking the dog or maybe strolling through the mall.

Look for the quarter when you are walking. Every time you are taking a walk, visualize the quarter.

How long did it take you to find the quarter?

Week Twelve

There can be nothing except as there is an idea, or ideal form, engendered in the Mind. Such ideas acting upon the Universal engender corresponding forms.

—Charles F. Haanel, *Master Key Arcana*

Week Thirteen

The Dreams of the Dreamer

The Letter of Transmittal

Physical science is responsible for the marvelous age of invention in which we are now living, but spiritual science is now setting out on a career whose possibilities no one can foretell.

Spiritual science has heretofore been the football of the uneducated, the superstitious, the mystical, but men are now interested in definite methods and demonstrated facts only.

We have come to know that thinking is a spiritual process, that vision and imagination precede action and event—that the day of the dreamer has come. The following lines by Mr. Herbert Kaufman are interesting in this connection.

"They are the architects of greatness, their vision lies within their souls, they peer beyond the veils and mists of doubt and pierce the walls of unborn Time. The belted wheel, the trail of steel, the churning screw, are shuttles in the loom on which they weave their magic tapestries. Makers of Empire, they have fought for bigger things than crowns and higher seats than thrones. Your homes are set upon the land a dreamer found. The pictures on its walls are visions from a dreamer's soul.

"They are the chosen few—the blazers of the way. Walls crumble and Empires fall, the tidal wave sweeps from the sea and tears a fortress from its rocks. The rotting nations drop from off Time's bough, and only things the dreamers make live on."

Week Thirteen which is enclosed herewith tells why the dreams of the dreamer come true. It explains the law of causation by which dreamers, inventors, authors, and financiers, bring about the realization of their desires. It explains the law by which the thing pictured upon our mind eventually becomes our own.

To observe individual facts carefully, patiently, accurately, with all the instruments and resources at their command, before venturing upon a statement of general laws is the method that natural philosophers use to obtain and apply their knowledge.

We may be certain that this method is correct by not permitting a tyrannical prejudice to neglect or mutilate unwelcome facts.

The class of facts esteemed most highly are those that cannot be accounted for by the usual daily observations of life.

This principle is founded upon reason and experience.

This principle destroys superstition, precedent, and conventionality.

These laws have been discovered by a generalization of facts that are uncommon, rare, strange, and form the exception.

The creative power of thought accounts for much of the strange and heretofore unexplainable phenomena that constantly takes place.

This is so because when we learn of a fact we can be sure that it is the result of a certain definite cause and that this cause will operate with invariable precision.

The result of this knowledge will explain the cause of every possible condition, whether physical, mental, or spiritual.

Our best interest will be conserved by a recognition of the fact that a knowledge of the creative nature of thought puts us in touch with Infinite power.

The Exercise

We can best conserve our interests by recognizing the Infinite Power and Infinite Wisdom of the Universal Mind, and in this way become a channel whereby the Infinite can bring about the realization of our desire. This means that recognition brings about realization. Therefore for your exercise this week make use of the principle. Recognize the fact that you are a part of the whole, and that a part must be the same in kind and quality as the whole; the only difference there can possibly be is in degree.

When this tremendous fact begins to permeate your consciousness, when you really come into a realization of the fact that you, not your body, but the Ego, the "I," the spirit which thinks, is an integral part of the great whole, that it is the same in substance, in quality, in kind, that the Creator could create nothing different from Himself, you will also be able to say, "The Father and I are one" and you will come into an understanding of the beauty, the grandeur, the transcendental opportunities which have been placed at your disposal.

Doing It

Failure is only postponed success as long as courage coaches ambition. The habit of persistence is the habit of victory.

—Herbert Kaufman

We can only achieve in life as we are willing to do. With *The Master Key System*, we are preparing our mind and learning how the Universal works. It is up to you, though, to put everything into practice. One cannot sit idly and wait for anything to drop into his lap. He must strike when the iron is hot; he must act when called to act; he must recognize opportunity when it arises.

...In Mysterious Ways

It was raining for a great many days and the river was beginning to flood. The people of the town went house to house requesting that everyone evacuate. They approached the house of Stan, a man of great faith in the Lord. When they asked him to come with them, he said, "I will stay here. I have faith in the Lord. He will protect me."

It continued to rain and the waters got higher and higher, high enough that the first floor of Stan's house was flooded. Rescue men came in a boat and asked Stan to come with them. Stan replied, "No need, my friends. The Lord will take care of me."

The waters got higher yet and Stan had to get onto his roof lest he perish. A helicopter came to rescue him, but Stan yelled, "No need! I have faith in the Lord and He will look after me."

Stan drowned. When he got to Heaven he was pretty angry. He immediately told Saint Peter to get the Lord so that they could talk. When the Lord appeared, He asked, "Stan, what are you doing here?"

"I should be asking You the same thing, Lord. I had great faith in You, but You let me drown in the flood!"

"Let you drown in the flood?" the Lord replied. "What do you mean? I sent a rescue team, a boat, and a helicopter to save you..."

Week Thirteen

A Key Point

> **Thought will create nothing unless it is consciously, systematically, and constructively directed. Herein is the difference between idle thinking, which is simply a dissipation of effort, and constructive thinking, which means practically unlimited achievement.**

Are you a few quarters wealthier now? You should be. Here is the question: Were those quarters always there or did they materialize because of your thoughts?

In the end, it does not matter, because in a sense it is the same thing. If you do not notice something and then one day you realize it's there, then it materialized in your life. Sure, it did not materialize in the "magical" sense of the word, but it came into being in your objective reality. You opened your perception to allow yourself to see them.

In a way, that is how the Law of Attraction works. **As we temper our mind and thoughts to things that are positive and beneficial to us, we open our eyes to those opportunities.** Perhaps those opportunities were there all along! How many times have you said that you wished you bought shares in Microsoft in 1986?

What do you have right now in your life that is an opportunity that you are overlooking? Center your thoughts on ones of abundance and opportunity, then examine your life. Can that vacant lot that you pass on your way to work be a good site for a gas station? Can an acquaintance help you get employment at a better company for a better wage? Enter the Silence. Envision positive thoughts. Make a list of the opportunities that are right under your nose.

1.

2.

3.

4.

5.

We are entitled to the best of everything. Pluck the fruit from the tree!

Our remedies in ourselves do lie
Which we ascribe to heaven.

—Shakespeare, *All's Well That Ends
Well*

Week Fourteen

The Creative Power of Thought

***The Letter of
Transmittal***

You have found from your study thus far that thought is a spiritual activity and is therefore endowed with creative power. This does not mean that some thought is creative, but that all thought is creative. This same principle can be brought into operation in a negative way through the process of denial.

The conscious and subconscious are but two phases of action in connection with one mind. The relation of the subconscious to the conscious is quite analogous to that existing between a weather vane and the atmosphere. Just as the least pressure of the atmosphere causes an action on the part of the weather vane, so does the least thought entertained by the conscious mind produce within your subconscious mind action in exact proportion to the depth of feeling characterizing the thought and the intensity with which the thought is indulged.

It follows that if you deny unsatisfactory conditions, you are withdrawing the creative power of your thought from these conditions. You are cutting them away at the root. You are sapping their vitality.

Remember that the law of growth necessarily governs every manifestation in the objective, so that a denial of unsatisfactory conditions will not bring about instant change. A plant will remain visible for some time after its roots have been cut, but it will gradually fade away and eventually disappear. So the withdrawal of your thought from the contemplation of unsatisfactory conditions will gradually but surely terminate these conditions.

You will see that this is an exactly opposite course from the one which we would naturally be inclined to adopt. It will therefore have an exactly opposite effect to the one usually secured. Most persons concentrate intently upon unsatisfactory conditions, thereby giving the condition that measure of energy and vitality which is necessary in order to supply a vigorous growth.

The source of all Wisdom, Power, and Intelligence is the Universal Mind.   ***The Main Points***

Motion, light, heat, and colour have their origin in the Universal Energy, which is one manifestation of the Universal Mind.

The creative power of thought also originates in the Universal Mind.

Thought is mind in motion.

The individual is the means by which the Universal produces the various combinations taht result in the formation of phenomena.

The power of the individual ot think is his ability to act upon the Universal and bring it into manifestation.

The first form that the Universal takes is electrons, which fill all space.

All things have their origin in mind.

A change of thought will result in a change of conditions.

A harmonious mental attitude will yield harmonious conditions in life.

For your exercise this week, concentrate on Harmony, and when I say   ***The Exercise***
concentrate, I mean all that the word implies—concentrate so deeply, so earnestly, that you will be conscious of nothing but Harmony. Remember, we learn by doing. Reading these lessons will get you nowhere. It is in the practical application that the value consists.

Week Fourteen

It Takes Some
Doing

Discipline is the fuel of achievement. Creativity sparks the flame, passion fans the fire, and discipline keeps it going for as long as it takes.

Disciplining yourself can be tedious, annoying, inconvenient and even agonizing. And yet, the results brought about by self-discipline cannot be reached in any other way. Discipline puts your most incredible dreams within reach. With self-discipline, you can make the best of your possibilities come to life. But how do you bring yourself to that level of discipline? You get there by knowing what you absolutely must do, and knowing that through self-discipline you can make it happen. What do you know in your heart that you are truly meant to accomplish? When you experience life as a mission, the discipline you need will be there.

Discipline and focus, applied consistently over time, can take you to truly amazing places. Where is it that you are uniquely suited to go?

—Ralph Marston

Week
Fourteen

A Key Point

> # Do what you are afraid to do.
> # Go where you are afraid to go.

Doing the
Exercise

Harmony is our natural state. Anything else, such as sickness, misfortune, or lack, is unnatural. Many have that reversed. They believe that it is normal to be imperfect. "To err is human" is what people commonly chant. By training one's mind, one will come to realize that a normal state is one of perfection and harmony. Only when he slips from his seat of perfection is he unnatural.

This week, you are to apply a method that will free you of lingering bad feelings that are caused by people or events in your past. Perhaps you harbor ill thoughts because you were scorned by a lover or maybe there was a family dispute. Whatever the cause, by carrying the thoughts with you, you continue to live the effects. Here is the method of dispelling those thoughts.

1. Forgive

2. Forget

That's it.

We must forgive those who wronged us and then forget about it. Now, that is not to say that we have to allow that person into our life again. It does not mean that we forget what we learned from that experience. That would make us fools. What we must do is merely move ahead.

For far too long there has been a plethora of psycho-babble and mollycoddling about things that happened to a person five, ten, fifty years ago. We are barraged daily by "pop" psychology terms like "baggage", "inner child", "closure", and other such nonsense. People continue to live in the past rather than progress with their life.

That is not to say that we shouldn't learn from experiences. We should learn all that we can from an experience so that we don't repeat the same mistake! That is not to say that if something traumatic happened that one shouldn't seek professional help. Remember, though, that the help should be that which helps you to progress, not relive or "deal".

This week, think of those people or events that bring a bad feeling to you. Perhaps you had a friend who wronged you badly. Forgive them. Then, forget about it. Drop the issue like you would drop a rock into a lake. (You can actually visualize yourself doing that. It will help. Imagine that the rock is your issue and visualize yourself dropping it into a lake. Watch it make a splash and then descend to the bottom until you cannot even see it anymore.)

It is most important that you do this. How many thoughts do you carry with you that are worthless and bring you nothing but bad feelings and therefore bad results? Keep in mind the tale of the two monks who helped the girl cross the muddy road. Leave her there! Likewise, leave your problems and issues behind you.

Today is Now and is the perfect time to begin living the rest of your life.

Here & Now

For this little exercise, we are going to concentrate on your "here and now." Take a few moments and think about your current situation. Now, make a list of all your tangible needs or things that are needed to satisfy your current requirements. A few examples are auto repairs, new clothes, bills to pay, and things of that nature.

This list is for the little things, not the things that are in your grand plan. Think along the lines of your monthly overhead. Not to confuse you, though, don't limit it to what you already have. Also include the things you would want or need right now. Don't think in a limited manner based upon past conditioning. Have fun! Don't worry about the money. Just list your tangible needs. Remember to be specific when listing them.

I need...

1.

2.

3.

4.

5.

6.

7.

8.

9.

10.

We are what we think. All that we are arises with our thoughts. With our thoughts, we make our world.

—Buddha

Week Fourteen

Week Fifteen

The Law Under Which We Live

The Letter of Transmittal

Dear Friend:
Experiments with parasites found on plants indicate that even the lowest order of life is enabled to take advantage of natural law.

This experiment was made by Jaques Loeb, M.D., Ph.D., a member of the Rockefeller Institute.

"In order to obtain the material, potted rose bushes are brought into a room and placed in front of a closed window. If the plants are allowed to dry out, the aphides (parasites), previously wingless, change to winged insects. After the metamorphosis, the animals leave the plants, fly to the window and then creep upward on the glass."

It is evident that these tiny insects found that the plants on which they had been thriving were dead, and that they could therefore secure nothing more to eat and drink from this source. The only method by which they could save themselves from starvation was to grow temporary wings and fly, which they did.

Experiments such as these indicate that Omniscience as well as Omnipotence is omnipresent and that the tiniest living thing can take advantage of it in an emergency.

Week Fifteen will tell you more about the law under which we live. It will explain that these laws operate to our advantage; that all conditions and experiences that come to us are for our benefit; that we gain strength in proportion to the effort expended; and that our happiness is best attained through a conscious cooperation with natural laws.

Our ability to appropriate what we require for our growth from each experience determines the degree of harmony that we attain.

Difficulties and obstacles are necessary for our wisdom and spiritual growth.

These difficulties may be avoided by a conscious understanding of and co-operation with Natural Laws.

The Law of Attraction is the principle by which thought manifests itself in form.

The necessary material by which the growth, development, and maturity of the idea take form is secured by the Law of Love, which is the creative principle of the Universe. The Law of Love imparts vitality to the thought and the Law of Attraction brings the necessary substance by the Law of Growth.

Desirable conditions are secured by entertaining desirable thoughts only.

Undesirable conditions are brought about by thinking, discussing, and visualizing conditions of lack, limitation, disease, inharmony, and discord of every kind. This mental photography of erroneous conceptions is taken up by the subconscious and the Law of Attraction will inevitably crystallize it into objective form. That we reap what we sow is scientifically exact.

We can overcome every kind of fear, lack, limitation, poverty, and discord by substituting principle for error.

We recognize principle by a conscious realization of the fact that Truth invariably destroys error. We do not have to laboriously shove the darkness out. All that is necessary is to turn on the light. The same principle applies to every form of negative thought.

Insight enables us to understand the value of making application of knowledge that we gain. Many seem to think that knowledge will automatically apply itself, which is by no means true.

The Main Points

For your exercise this week, concentrate on Insight. Take your accustomed position and focus the thought on the fact that to have a knowledge of the creative power of thought does not mean to possess the art of thinking. Let the thought dwell on the fact that knowledge does not apply itself. That our actions are not governed by knowledge, but by custom, precedent, and habit. That the only way we can get ourselves to apply knowledge is by a determined conscious effort. Call to mind the fact that knowledge unused passes from the mind, that the value of the information is in the application of the principle. Continue this line of thought until you gain sufficient insight to formulate a definite program for applying this principle to your own particular problem.

The Exercise

Week Fifteen

Look Similar?

The pathway to salvation is as narrow and as difficult to walk as a razor's edge.

—Tibetan Monk, *The Razor's Edge*
(1984)

There is a principle of Mathematics, but none of error; there is a principle of health, but none of disease; there is a principle of truth, but none of dishonesty; there is a principle of light, but none of darkness; and there is a principle of abundance, but none of poverty.

—Charles F. Haanel, *The Master Key System*

When Things
Don't Add Up

$$a + b = 2$$
$$a + b \neq 2$$

Examine the two equations that appear here. If we are working with positive whole numbers (that is, numbers that are positive and do not have any fractions associated with them), then it is quite easy to solve the first equation. The solution is, of course, "1 + 1 = 2".

The second equation, though, becomes more difficult. Just about any two numbers other than 1 and 1 will not equal 2. Thus, there is a veritable infinity of numbers that will not equal 2.

What does this illustrate? In life, it is the positive that can be proved by a certain, definable method or way. If you ask me for directions to my house, then I can give them to you very easily. I can also tell you how not to get here, but that would take considerably longer.

Likewise, you can tell me a plethora of ways not to bake a cake; whereas there is only one way to make a certain kind of cake. Your recipe is your way, your method, for baking the cake. Any other way I bake the cake will not result in your cake.

As you read *The Master Key System*, keep this principle in mind. This is the method by which one will accomplish wonders and seeming miracles. You can do whatever you may to escape debt or build a relationship, but without these principles to support your efforts, you are building a castle of sand on a beach where the tide is quickly rising.

aanel lists for us the three laws that are Natural Laws that are working for us. Let's review them one at a time and work to put them into practice.

1. The Law of Attraction
We attract to us the things, people, and circumstances that we think about. If we desire a new house and we visualize the house we desire in complete, definite, and unvarying detail, then we will set into motion the things necessary for us to attain that house.

2. The Law of Love
As we visualize, we will attain only so much as we infuse our thoughts with positive and vibrant emotions. "Believe that ye receive and ye shall receive." Our level of faith and confidence in attaining our goal will determine how quickly and how thoroughly that goal comes to pass.

3. The Law of Growth
We shall reap what we sow and as we think and believe we will encounter in life. As we encounter difficulties, we add to our wisdom when we overcome them. We replace old modes of thinking for new ones, thus paving the way for bigger and better things.

> **Growth is attained through an exchange of the old for the new, of the good for the better...We cannot attain what we lack if we tenaciously cling to what we have.**

For this week, in addition to the usual weekly exercise that Haanel outlines, let us practice a method of growing that works wonders. When you are done, you will have replaced the good with the better.

Look around your house and take notice of the things that could be replaced. Let us use as an example your drapes. If they are in need of replacing, then simply get rid of them! Do not sell them or try to make money from the transaction, merely give them to a charitable organization, such as The Salvation Army. By making the path clear for the better to enter, the better will arrive.

You can go even further and do a thorough house cleaning. This will unburden you of much of your baggage and clear the way for new and better things. It is not advocated to dispose things of value, but the general rule is that if you haven't looked at a thing in many years, then it can go,

*Rewriting your
story*

Week
Fifteen

In order that the spirit may convey wisdom to the mind, it is important that you have a special time for quietness or silence in which you should allow no interruptions.

—Charles F. Haanel, *The Amazing Secrets of the Yogi*

**Remember!
Take time each day to enter the Silence.**

The Master Key Workbook

94

Week Sixteen

Gaining Spiritual Understanding

***The Letter of
Transmittal***

The vibratory activities of the planetary Universe are governed by a law of periodicity. Everything that lives has periods of birth, growth, fruitage, and decline. These periods are governed by the Septimal Law.

The Law of Sevens governs the days of the week, the phases of the moon, the harmonies of sound, light, heat, electricity, magnetism, atomic structure. It governs the life of individuals and of nations, and it dominates the activities of the commercial world.

Life is growth and growth is change. Each seven year period takes us into a new cycle. The first seven years is the period of infancy. The next seven the period of childhood, representing the beginning of individual responsibility. The next seven represents the period of adolescence. The fourth period marks the attainment of full growth. The fifth period is the constructive period, when men begin to acquire property, possessions, a home, and family. The next from 35 to 42, is a period of reactions and changes, and this in turn is followed by a period of reconstruction, adjustment, and recuperation, so as to be ready for a new cycle of sevens, beginning with the fiftieth year.

There are many who think that the world is just about to pass out of the sixth period; that it will soon enter into the seventh period, the period of readjustment, reconstruction, and harmony; the period which is frequently referred to as the Millennium.

Those familiar with these cycles will not be disturbed when things seem to go wrong, but can apply the principle outlined in these lessons with the full assurance that a higher law will invariably control all other laws, and that through an understanding and conscious operation of spiritual laws, we can convert every seeming difficulty into a blessing.

Wealth depends upon an understanding of the creative nature of thought.   *The Main Points*

True value consists of its exchange value.

Success depends upon spiritual power.

Spiritual power depends upon use. Use determines its existence.

We may take our fate out of the hands of chance by consciously realizing the conditions that we desire to see manifested in our lives.

Thinking is the greatest business of life because thought is spiritual and therefore creative. To consciously control thought is therefore to control circumstances, conditions, environment, and destiny.

Destructive thinking is the source of all evil.

Scientific correct thinking is the source of all good.

Scientific thinking is a recognition of the creative nature of spiritual energy and our ability to control it.

For your exercise this week, try to bring yourself to a realization of the   *The Exercise*
important fact that harmony and happiness are states of consciousness and do not depend upon the possession of things. Realize that things are effects and come as a consequence of correct mental states. So that if we desire material possession of any kind our chief concern should be to acquire the mental attitude which will bring about the result desired. This mental attitude is brought about by a realization of our spiritual nature and our unity with the Universal Mind, which is the substance of all things. This realization will bring about everything which is necessary for our complete enjoyment. This is scientific or correct thinking. When we succeed in bringing about this mental attitude it is comparatively easy to realize our desire as an already accomplished fact; when we can do this we shall have found the "Truth" which makes us "free" from every lack or limitation of any kind.

Who Is That Guy?

Venture capitalist and Forbes columnist Guy Kawasaki was recently interviewed about his book, *The Art of the Start*. Here is a snippet from that interview.

PAUL MAIDMENT: Guy, you have a Top Five list of things an entrepreneur must accomplish. At the top of that list is Make Meaning. What does that mean, and why is it so important?

GUY KAWASAKI: It means that if you start a company to "make money" then you'll probably fail. Great companies start because the founders want to change the world ... not make a fast buck. Call me a romantic, but I think entrepreneurs should try to change the world. This comes from working at Apple ... old habits die hard.

MAIDMENT: Is there ever a case in which 'making yourself rich' constitutes making meaning?

KAWASAKI: Yes, absolutely. But that seems like an insipid reason to start a company. However, if you make meaning, you'll probably make money. If you make money, you might not make meaning. At the end of one's life, hopefully you've done more than simply make money.

It would behoove us to listen to that guy.

Why?

Wealth is a by-product of or a means to a noble end. It should not be confused with your *raison de vivre* or your chief aim. The greatest men in the world sought nobler ends. Did Edison profit from his inventions? Yes, he did. His love for discovery came first, though. The money followed.

So it continues with every great person who does great things.

There is something that exists that is greater than wealth or acclaim. That something is your **Why**. Why are you doing something? What is your ideal? Why?

Think about why you want certain things. Is it because you wish to show-off? Is it to gain revenge? Or is it for lofty reasons? Or simply to be the best at what you do?

Ask yourself *Why?*. Know thyself!

If your thought is constructive, it will possess vitality and it will grow, develop, and expand. It will attract everything necessary for its development.

> **Good and evil therefore are not entities, they are simply words that we use to indicate the result of our actions, and these actions are in turn predetermined by the character of our thoughts.**

Say It with Feeling

As we have discussed before, it is imperative to put the Law of Love into motion by imbuing your thoughts with feeling. Haanel conveniently provides an explanation for us:

> The psychologists have come to the conclusion that there is but one sense, the sense of feeling, and that all other senses are but modifications of this one sense. This being true, we know why feeling is the fountain-head of power, why the emotions so easily overcome the intellect, and why we must put feelings into our thought if we wish results. Thought and feeling is the irresistible combination.

Be certain to refer to the goals you have written, imagine yourself already possessing them or attaining them, and do that with feeling. Cultivate and feel feelings of strength, courage, pride, integrity, and love.

Write a few sentences about how attaining your goals would make you feel. Include why you would feel that way. For example, you may write, "I would feel happy and proud to receive a promotion at work because then I would be able to afford a better education for my son."

Week Sixteen

"You seek escape from pain. We seek the achievement of happiness. You exist for the sake of avoiding punishment. We exist for the sake of earning rewards. Threats will not make us function; fear is not our incentive. It is not death that we wish to avoid, but life that we wish to live."

—Ayn Rand, *Atlas Shrugged*

Week Seventeen

Symbols and Reality

***The Letter of
Transmittal***

The kind of Deity which a man, consciously or unconsciously, worships indicates the intellectual status of the worshipper. Ask the Indian of God and he will describe to you a powerful chieftain of a glorious tribe. Ask the Pagan of God and he will tell you of a God of fire, a God of water, a God of this, that, and the other.

Ask the Israelite of God and he will tell you of the God of Moses, who conceived it expedient to rule by coercive measures; hence, the Ten Commandments. Or of Joshua, who led the Israelites into battle, confiscated property, murdered the prisoners, and laid waste to cities.

The so-called heathen made "graven images" of their Gods, whom they were accustomed to worship, but among the most intelligent, at least, these images were but the visible fulcrums with which they were enabled to mentally concentrate on the qualities which they desired to externalize in their lives.

We of the twentieth century worship a God of Love in theory but in practice we make for ourselves "graven images" of "Wealth," "Power," "Fashion," "Custom," and "Conventionality." We "fall down" before them and worship them. We concentrate on them and they are thereby externalized in our lives.

The student who masters the contents of Week Seventeen will not mistake the symbols for the reality; he will be interested in causes, rather than effects. He will concentrate on the realities of life and will then not be disappointed in the results.

The true method of concentration is to become so identified with the object of your thought that you are conscious of nothing else.

The result of this method of concentration is that invisible forces are set in motion that irresistibly bring about conditions in correspondence with your thoughts.

Spiritual Truth is the controlling factor in this method of thought because the nature of our desire must be in harmony with Natural Law.

The practical value of this method of concentration is that thought is transmuted into character, and character is the magnet that creates the environment of the individual.

The mental element is the controlling factor in any commercial pursuit because mind is the ruler and creator of all form and all events occurring in form.

Concentration operates by the development of the powers of perception, wisdom, intuition, and sagacity.

Intuition is superior to reason because it does not depend upon experience or memory and frequently brings about the solution to our problem by methods concerning which we are in entire ignorance.

When we pursue the symbols of reality, the symbols frequently turn to ashes just as we overtake them, because the symbol is only the outward form of the spiritual activity within. Therefore, unless we can possess the spiritual reality, the form disappears.

For your exercise this week concentrate as nearly as possible in accordance with the method outlined in this lesson. Let there be no conscious effort or activity associated with your purpose. Relax completely and avoid any thought of anxiety as to results. Remember that power comes through repose. Let the thought dwell upon your object until it is completely identified with it, until you are conscious of nothing else.

If you wish to eliminate fear, then concentrate on courage.

If you wish to eliminate lack, then concentrate on abundance.

If you wish to eliminate disease, then concentrate on health.

Always concentrate on the ideal as an already existing fact. This is the Elohim, the germ cell, the life principle which goes forth and enters in and becomes, sets in motion those causes which guide, direct, and bring about the necessary relation, which eventually manifest in form.

You²

Price Pritchett relates a wonderful story in his book, *You²*. He tells the tale of a fly trying to escape from his motel room. The fly is scrambling and trying with all of its might to get through the glass of the windowpane. While the fly is trying harder and harder to escape its confines, not more than ten feet away, the door is open.

All of the effort in the world would yield but a fraction of what mental effort can. **Worker smarter** is the new axiom!

Concentration is the key to this. As you allow your mind to dwell on a single goal rather than scattering its energy, you will find doors open that weren't even there before.

A Key Point

> **Every obstacle conquered, every victory gained, will give you more faith in your power, and you will have greater ability to win.**

The Taste of Banzo's Sword

Matajuro Yagyu was the son of a famous swordsman. His father, disowned him because his work was not very good. Matajuro then sought Banzo, the famous swordsman, in hopes that he would teach him.

"How many years will it take me to become a master?" asked the youth.

"The rest of your life," replied Banzo.

Matajuro was told never to speak of fencing and never to touch a sword. He cooked for his master, washed the dishes, made the bed, cleaned the yard, tended the garden, all without a word of swordsmanship.

Three years passed and Matajuro labored on. He was sad because he had not even begun to learn the art to which he had devoted his life.

One day, Banzo crept up behind him as he worked and gave him a terrific blow with a wooden sword. The following day, when Matajuro was cooking rice, Banzo again sprang upon him unexpectedly.

After that, day and night, Matajuro had to defend himself against unexpected thrusts. Not a moment passed every day that he was safe from Banzo's sword. He learned so rapidly that he brought smiles to the face of his master. Matajuro eventually became the greatest swordsman in the land.

As you prepare to concentrate this week, make a list for yourself of the things that you wish to conquer, such as fear or envy. Be specific when you make your list. You will put this list on the left-hand column.

You will use the right-hand column to list the opposite of what you have written. This will help you to concentrate on what you want, rather than on what you do not want. For example, on the left you may write "I am broke." On the right, you will write, "I have a positive cash flow."

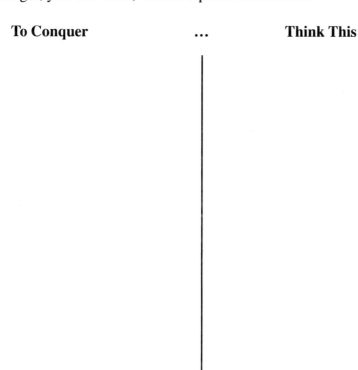

To Conquer   ...   **Think This**

These exercises are your training—your Banzo's sword. Every day, we are barraged by thoughts and self-talk, some of which is negative and unproductive. They come unbidden and seemingly from nowhere. Unexpectedly, they spring into our heads and attempt to foil the attainment of our goals, dreams, and ideals.

It is the aim of these exercises to have you ready like Matajuro in the tale that you read. When a thought that does not help you arises, you will immediately be ready to block it and nullify it. Only by practice and repetition will you be able to do that. Once it is set, though, you will be ready to deal with even the most negative of thoughts because your mind will be strong and you will know how to live from the Truth.

A Zen Tale

Two monks were travelling together down a muddy road. It was raining heavily. They met a lovely girl on the road who was unable to cross the intersection because the mud would ruin her silk kimono. One of the monks lifted the girl in his arms and carried her over the mud.

Later that evening, when the monks were in their lodgings, the other monk said to the one who carried the girl, "We monks do not go near females! Especially not young, pretty ones. It is dangerous. Why did you do that?"

The other monk replied, "I left the girl there. Are you still carrying her?"

Week Eighteen

The Law of Attraction

***The Letter of
Transmittal***

In order to grow we must obtain what is necessary for our growth. This is brought about through the law of attraction. This principle is the sole means by which the individual is differentiated from the Universal.

Think for a moment. What would a man be if he were not a husband, a father, or a brother; if he were not interested in the social, economical, political, or religious world? He would be nothing but an abstract theoretical ego. He exists, therefore, only in his relation to the whole, in his relation to other men, in his relation to society. This relation constitutes his environment. He exists therefore in his relation to his environment and in no other way.

It is evident, therefore, that the individual is simply the differentiation of the one Universal Mind "which lighteth every man that cometh into the world," and his so-called individuality or personality consists of nothing but the manner in which he relates with the whole.

This we call his environment and is brought about by the law of attraction. Week Eighteen, which I enclose herewith, has something more to say concerning this important law.

The difference in individual lives is measured by the degree of intelligence that they manifest.

By a recognition of the self as an individualization of the Universal Intelligence the individual may control other forms of intelligence.

The creative power originates in the Universal.

The Universal creates form by means of the individual.

Thought is the connecting link between the individual and the Universal.

The Law of Love is the principle by which the means of existence is carried to effect.

The Law of Growth brings this principle into expression.

The Law of Growth depends upon reciprocal action. The individual is complete at all times and this makes it possible to receive only as we give.

What we give is thought.

We receive thought, which is substance in equilibrium and which is constantly being differentiated in form by what we think.

This week concentrate upon your power to create. Seek insight and perception. Try to find a logical basis for the faith which is in you. Let the thought dwell on the fact that the physical man lives and moves and has his being in the sustainer of all organic life air, that he must breathe to live. Then let the thought rest on the fact that the spiritual man also lives and moves and has his being in a similar but subtler energy upon which he must depend for life, and that as in the physical world no life assumes form until after a seed is sown, and no higher fruit than that of the parent stock can be produced; so in the spiritual world no effect can be produced until the seed is sown and the fruit will depend upon the nature of the seed, so that the results which you secure depend upon your perception of law in the mighty domain of causation, the highest evolution of human consciousness.

Pay Attention!

In order to take advantage of the Law of Attraction to the fullest, one must be able to keep one's attention on the goal. One must be able to hold the vision unwaveringly. Thoughts of abundance will attract money and opportunity. Thoughts of love will bring harmony. Thoughts of power will yield self-sufficiency.

The attention can be trained. That is what the exercises in *The Master Key System* are doing for you. You are able to keep your mind focused like a laser. As you hold your attention and keep it focused, you will be attracting to you the things, people, and circumstances that you need for your growth.

A Key Point

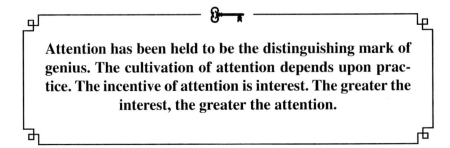

Attention has been held to be the distinguishing mark of genius. The cultivation of attention depends upon practice. The incentive of attention is interest. The greater the interest, the greater the attention.

Be Here Now

How do we keep the mind from wandering, though? How do we still those voices that remind us of the past and worry us with the future? As Haanel would say, it is by practice that we gain control of our mind. That is the only way. It won't hurt, though, to take a closer look at what is happening.

A weird fellow by the name of Baba Ram Dass wrote a book entitled *Be Here Now*. In it, he explains that we must take advantage of the moment and not let the mind drift from it. How many times have you missed something that was occurring because your mind was elsewhere? Perhaps you missed your son get a base-hit because you were worrying about a project at work. Mayhap you were having money troubles and did not allow yourself to fully enjoy the holidays.

Most times, you do not even feel your mind drift. You only realize that you were "in your own little world" when you have to ask someone to repeat something or you have to act like you just saw what occurred. A good clue that you are not there mentally is that your body starts doing its rhythmical tics, such as tapping your feet, shaking your leg, playing with your fingers, or any other of a number of somewhat annoying fidgets.

The Past		The Future
Shame		Worry
Nostalgia		Fear
Fear	**NOW**	Anxiety
Bad Programming		Wasteful thoughts

As you can see in the diagram, by allowing the mind to drift, you are essentially dissipating your mental energy and creating in yourself feelings that may not be in your best interest.

Many people dwell on the past. "It's not my fault, Your Honor. I had a bad childhood." Have you heard that before? How about "My mother was never there. She didn't love me enough." Have you heard a person explain with that excuse why they encounter one bad relationship after another?

Let go of the past. It is gone. Bring yourself into the Now. Why dwell on something that happened many years ago? If you've encountered failures, then try something new! The movie *Vanilla Sky* provides us with a wonderful thing to remember.

**Every passing minute is another chance
to turn it all around.**

What goes for the past is true of the future. If you are not making plans, then why are you worrying about the future? Worry and anxiety are some of the biggest wastes of mental energy. They cause us to fear and many times they throw us into a state of paralysis. Keep your thoughts courageous and in the *Now*. You will be happy that you did.

Y ou are not required to write much this week. The writing for this week consists of only three words.

Stay in the Now

BE HERE NOW

Get a few 3x5 cards and write "BE HERE NOW" on them. Place them where you can see them, places where it is easy for you to drift off. Common places are on your desk, on the visor of your car, and even by your television.

Keep yourself in the *Now*. When you notice your body fidgeting, ask yourself where you are. Look at the things around you. Notice something that you've not noticed before that moment.

Pay attention!

A poor student utilizes a teacher's influence.
A fair student admires a teacher's kindness.
A good student grows strong under a teacher's discipline.

—Zen Saying

Week Nineteen

Your Mental Food

*The Letter of
Transmittal*

Fear is a powerful form of thought. It paralyzes the nerve centers, thus affecting the circulation of the blood. This, in turn, paralyzes the muscular system, so that fear affects the entire being—body, brain and nerve, physical, mental, and muscular.

Of course, the way to overcome fear is to become conscious of power. What is this mysterious vital force which we call power? We do not know; neither do we know what electricity is. But we do know that by conforming to the requirements of the law by which electricity is governed, it will be our obedient servant; that it will light our homes, our cities, run our machinery, and serve us in many useful capacities.

And so it is with vital force. Although we do not know what it is, and possibly may never know, we do know that it is a primary force which manifests through living bodies, and that by complying with the laws and principles by which it is governed we can open ourselves to a more abundant inflow of this vital energy, and thus express the highest possible degree of mental, moral and spiritual efficiency.

The lesson which I enclose herewith tells of a very simple way of developing this vital force. If you put into practice the information outlined in this lesson you will soon develop the sense of power which has ever been the distinguishing mark of genius.

Extremes are designated by distinctive names, such as inside and outside, top and bottom, light and dark, good and bad. This is how they are placed in contrast.

The Main Points

They are not separate entities. They are parts, or aspects, of one Whole.

The Universal Mind, or the Eternal Energy, from which all things proceed is the one creative Principle in the physical, mental, and spiritual world.

We are related to this creative principle by our ability to think.

This creative principle becomes operative by thought. Thought is the seed, which results in action and action results in form.

Form depends upon the rate of vibration.

The rate of vibration may be changed by mental action.

Mental action depends upon polarity, action and reaction, between the individual and the Universal.

The creative energy originates in the Universal, but the Universal can only manifest through the individual.

The individual is necessary because the Universal is static and requires energy to start it in motion. This is furnished by food, which is converted into energy, which in turn enables the individual to think. When the individual stops eating he stops thinking; then he no longer acts upon the Universal; there is consequently no longer any action or reaction; the Universal is then only pure mind in static form. It is mind at rest.

For your exercise this week, concentrate, and when I use the word concentrate, I mean all that the word implies: Become so absorbed in the object of your thought that you are conscious of nothing else, and do this a few minutes every day. You take the necessary time to eat in order that the body may be nourished, why not take the time to assimilate your mental food?

The Exercise

Let the thought rest on the fact that appearances are deceptive. The earth is not flat, neither is it stationary; the sky is not a dome; the sun does not move; the stars are not small specks of light; and matter which was once supposed to be fixed has been found to be in a state of perpetual flux.

Try to realize that the day is fast approaching—its dawn is now at hand— when modes of thought and action must be adjusted to rapidly increasing knowledge of the operation of eternal principles.

Losing the Fear

Fear is something that must be destroyed. Living in fear or fearing things leads to mental dissipation on a massive level. This is the mental effort that will return to us the things that we do not want instead of the things that we do.

In *Master Key Arcana*, which contains the "lost" parts of *The Master Key System*, Haanel explains a method by which we can squash fear if we begin to feel it. Here is that method.

> Fear is an emotion. It is consequently not amenable to reason. You may therefore fear your friends as well as your enemies or fear the present and past as well as the future. If fear attacks you, it must be destroyed.

> You will be interested in knowing how to accomplish this. Reason will not help you at all, because fear is a subconscious thought—a product of the emotion. There must then be some other way.

> The way is to awaken the Solar Plexus. Get it into action. If you have practiced deep breathing, then you can expand the abdomen to the limit. That is the first thing to do. Hold this breath for a second or two, then still holding it, draw in more air and carry it to the upper chest and draw in the abdomen.

> This effort flushes the face red. Hold this breath also for a second or two and then, still holding your breath, deflate the chest and expand the abdomen again. Do not exhale this breath at all, but, still holding it, alternately expand the abdomen and chest rapidly some four or five times. Then exhale. The fear is gone.

> If the fear does not leave you at once, repeat the process until it does.

Practice this when you feel any amount of fear. As some like to say, "Nip it in the bud!" To learn more about breathing and the positive effects it can have, read Haanel's *The Amazing Secrets of the Yogi*.

I am fearless in my heart. They will always see that in my eyes! I am the passion; I am the warfare. I will never stop. Always constant, accurate, and intense.

—Steve Vai

Week Twenty

The Spirit of Things

**The Letter of
Transmittal**

For many years there has been an endless discussion as to the origin of evil. Theologians have told us that God is Love and that God is Omnipresent. If this be true, there is no place where God is not. Where, then, is Evil, Satan, and Hell? Let us see:

God is Spirit.

Spirit is the Creative Principle of the Universe.

Man is made in the image and likeness of God.

Man is therefore a spiritual being.

The only activity which spirit possesses is the power to think.

Thinking is therefore a creative process.

All form is therefore the result of the thinking process.

The destruction of form must also be a result of the thinking process.

Fictitious representations of form are the result of the creative power of thought, as in Hypnotism

Apparent representations of form are the result of the creative power of thought, as in Spiritualism.

Invention, organization, and constructive work of all kinds are the result of the creative power of thought, as in concentration.

When the creative power of thought is manifested for the benefit of humanity, we call the result good.

When the creative power of thought is manifested in a destructive or evil manner, we call the result evil.

This indicates the origin of both good and evil; they are simply words which have been coined in order to indicate the nature of the result of the thinking or creative process.

Thought necessarily precedes and predetermines action; action precedes and predetermines condition.

Week Twenty will throw more light upon this important subject.

Power depends upon recognition and use.   *The Main Points*

Recognition is consciousness.

We become conscious of power by thinking.

Correct scientific thinking is the true business of life.

Correct scientific thinking is the ability to adjust our thought processes to the will of the Universal. In other words, to cooperate with Natural Laws.

Correct scientific thinking is accomplished by securing a perfect understanding of the principles, forces, methods, and combinations of mind.

The Universal Mind is the basic fact of all existence.

All lack, limitation, disease, and discord are due to the operation of exactly the same law. The law operates relentlessly and is continually bringing about conditions in correspondence with the thought that originated or created them.

Inspiration is the art of realizing the omnipresence of Omniscience.

The conditions with which we meet depends upon the quality of our thought. Because what we do depends upon what we are and what we are depends upon what we think.

For your exercise this week, go into the Silence and concentrate on the fact   *The Exercise*
that "In Him we live and move and have our being" is literally and scientifically exact! That you ARE because He IS, that if He is Omnipresent He must be in you. That if He is all in all you must be in Him! That He is Spirit and you are made in "His image and likeness" and that the only difference between His spirit and your spirit is one of degree, that a part must be the same in kind and quality as the whole. When you can realize this clearly you will have found the secret of the creative power of thought, you will have found the origin of both good and evil, you will have found the secret of the wonderful power of concentration, you will have found the key to the solution of every problem whether physical, financial, or environmental.

***One Man's
Junk...***

You probably know that old adage, "One man's junk is another man's treasure." As a matter of fact, you have probably seen or heard about it in operation. Perhaps you've seen the television show where auction people appraise what appears to be junk. They startle the owners of the junk by informing them that in truth, the "junk" they possess is a valuable antique.

Closer to home, you've probably seen this adage in operation. How many times have you uttered "I thought of that" or "I could do that better" when you see a person making money with a product or service. In operation, the adage becomes "One man's junk is another man's fortune!"

Within you is untapped power. There is "junk" awaiting to be polished so that its true value can be ascertained. Your fortune is your mind! As you wait for things to happen for you, some one else is making things happen for them self. Why cannot you do the same?

The answer is simple: There is no reason why you cannot take advantage of your ideas. You must take action. To take action, you have to know what is in your inventory. This week, you will concentrate on what you have. From that point you can spring into action and turn your "junk" into your fortune.

A Key Point

> **You may have all the wealth in Christendom, but unless you recognize it and make use of it, it will have no value...All great things come through recognition.**

***Command
Yourself***

An inquirer asked a teacher, "How can I command whatever happens to me?"

"By being one with whatever happens."

"What does that mean?"

"You really do not possess a separate self which is apart from anything; you are one with all of life. However, in your misunderstanding you think there is a you **and** an event, which causes division and conflict. Give up your belief in a separate self and oneness will be realized, which ends conflict. This is the secret of the ages. Come back to it every day. You will change."

You become the commander of everything by not needing to command anything but yourself.

Yᵒu are going to do some writing this week. It's important that you take an inventory of what you have in order for you to recognize your potential. Just as we can fail to recognize our world within, we often fail to recognize the things that we have that can be worth a fortune to us. Since we do not recognize them, we do not exercise them. Hence, they go dormant and they atrophy. Take the time to make a full inventory of what you have. If you have to (and you probably will), get another sheet of paper.

Here you are to write the things you know like math or a language or even things like jokes. Just about anything you know.

Things I Know...

1.
2.
3.
4.
5.
6.
7.
8.
9.
10.

Write the things that you can do from the inane to the complex, anything from whistling to repairing a car to using a computer.

Things I Can Do...

1.
2.
3.
4.
5.
6.
7.
8.
9.
10.

Continued on the next page...

Death is nothing; but to live defeated and inglorious in to die daily.

—Napoleon

*Taking Stock
Continued...*

Make a list of things you practice daily, such as problem-solving or task management, the skills that you do, sort of without you even knowing it.

Things I Practice Daily...

1.
2.
3.
4.
5.
6.
7.
8.
9.
10.

Write a list of the things that people tell you that you do well. Maybe you hear that you're a good talker or you have a good sense of humour.

Things I Hear From People...

1.
2.
3.
4.
5.
6.
7.
8.
9.
10.

What do you own or have? Make a list of things that you have, such as a computer, a telephone, a house, or a musical instrument.

Things I Have...

1.
2.
3.
4.
5.
6.
7.
8.
9.
10.

Who do you know? Go through your Rolodex and compile a list of people you know. Maybe they can help you, maybe not. Let's put them on the list just the same.

*The Stock Taking
Continues...*

People I Know...

1.
2.
3.
4.
5.
6.
7.
8.
9.
10.

What jobs or occupations have you had? Butcher? Baker? Candlestick maker? Make that list here.

Jobs I Have Had...

1.
2.
3.
4.
5.
6.
7.
8.
9.
10.

What roles have you taken? Were you ever a Scout Leader or PTA Member? That list goes here.

Roles I Have Assumed...

1.
2.
3.
4.
5.
6.
7.
8.
9.
10.

Mix It All Together

Take a good look at your lists. Do you see any common threads? Do some things line up nicely? Perhaps you fix cars and you work in a shop and a lot of the people you know also fix cars. (If you are a mechanic that makes sense!) Perhaps you know computers and you work in an office; mayhap you can parlay that combination into a new and better job or a business.

The point is that by seeing everything on your list, you now know where you stand and you can go from there. Perhaps if you are a mechanic, you know a few other fellows who would be interested in opening a repair shop or customizing shop. You can see the basis for an idea and now you have the inventory to make it so.

If your lists do not seem to mesh well, perhaps you have to look closer and do a little pruning. Examine the lists and think about which items brought you the most pleasure and enjoyment. Maybe now you work in a stifling office, but you know a lot of jokes and people keep telling you that your a wonderful person with a great attitude; that might be indicative that you could really succeed in a sales position.

The last part is difficult. It may not be easy to see where to go, but at least now you know where you stand. Give this lots of thought. Put things together. You will then turn your "junk" into your fortune.

Do not think that you are on the right road just because it is a well-beaten path.

—Anonymous

Depend on the rabbit's foot if you will, but it didn't work for the rabbit!

—Anonymous

Week Twenty-One

To Think Big Thoughts

The Letter of Transmittal

It is my privilege to enclose Week Twenty-One. In paragraph seven you will find that one of the secrets of success, one of the methods of organizing victory, one of the accomplishments of the Master Mind, is to think big thoughts.

In paragraph eight you will find that everything which we hold in our consciousness for any length of time becomes impressed upon our subconsciousness and so becomes a pattern which the creative energy will weave into our life and environment. This is the secret of the wonderful power of prayer.

We know that the universe is governed by law; that for every effect there must be a cause; and that the same cause, under the same conditions, will invariably produce the same effect. Consequently, if prayer has ever been answered, it will always be answered if the proper conditions are complied with. This must necessarily be true. Otherwise, the universe would be a chaos instead of a cosmos. The answer to prayer is therefore subject to law and this law is definite, exact, and scientific, just as are the laws governing gravitation and electricity. An understanding of this law takes the foundation of Christianity out of the realm of superstition and credulity and places it upon the firm rock of scientific understanding.

But, unfortunately, there are comparatively few persons who know how to pray. They understand that there are laws governing electricity, mathematics, and chemistry, but, for some inexplicable reason, it never seems to occur to them that there are also spiritual laws and that these laws are also definite, scientific, exact, and operate with immutable precision.

The real secret of power is the consciousness of power, because whatever we become conscious of is invariably manifested in the objective world and is brought forth into tangible expression.

The source of this power is the Universal Mind, from which all things proceed and which is one and indivisible.

This power is being manifested through the individual. Each individual is a channel whereby this energy is being differentiated in form.

Our ability to think is our ability to act on this Universal Energy and what we think is what is produced or created in the objective world. The result of this discovery is nothing less than marvelous. It opens unprecedented and limitless opportunity.

We may eliminate imperfect conditions by becoming conscious of our unity with the source of all power.

One of the distinctive characteristics of the Master Mind is that he thinks big thoughts. He holds ideas large enough to counteract and destroy all petty and annoying obstacles.

Experiences come to us through the law of attraction.

Our predominant mental attitude brings this law into operation.

The issue between the old regime and the new is a question of conviction as to the nature of the Universe. The old regime is trying to cling to the fatalistic doctrine of Divine election. The new regime recognizes the divinity of the individual and the democracy of humanity.

The Main Points

For your exercise this week, concentrate on the Truth. Try to realize that the Truth shall make you free. That is, nothing can permanently stand in the way of your perfect success when you learn to apply the scientifically correct thought methods and principles. Realize that you are externalizing in your environment your inherent soul potencies. Realize that the Silence offers an ever available and almost unlimited opportunity for awakening the highest conception of Truth. Try to comprehend that Omnipotence itself is absolute silence—all else is change, activity, limitation. Silent thought concentration is therefore the true method of reaching, awakening, and then expressing the wonderful potential power of the world within.

The Exercise

It Bears Repeating...

It was stated previously in this workbook that one of Donald Trump's rules is to "Think big." Obviously, thinking big worked well for him. Bill Gates, too, thinks big. When he began Microsoft, the company motto was "A computer on every desktop." Now that they have a virtual monopoly of computer operating systems, that motto came to fruition.

Throughout history, you'll find that those who get mentioned in the history books or are remembered, were those who held big thoughts in their mind and endeavoured to make them real. Alexander the Great, Napoleon, John F. Kennedy. These men dared to dream.

What are your dreams? Whatever they are, make them lofty and grand. Shoot for the Moon! As the saying goes, even if you miss the Moon, maybe you'll hit a star.

The Process

"**The real secret of power is consciousness of power.**" Haanel implores us to use this power as it is what brings into reality the thoughts that we have, be those thoughts for good or for ill. To ensure that the results we get are the ones that we desire, Haanel has this process for us. Use it!

1. Every thought creates an impression on the brain.
2. Experiences come to us through the law of attraction.
3. The predominant thought or mental attitude is the magnet.
4. Like attracts like.
5. The mental attitude is our personality and is composed of all the thoughts that we have been creating in our mind.
6. By persistent effort, we can change the mental attitude.
7. To do this, replace the pictures you have in your mind with new pictures of what you want and desire.
8. When you have done this, you will begin to attract to yourself those things.
9. Build into your mental pictures the necessary essentials, such as determination, ability, talent, courage, power, and anything else.
10. Aspire to the highest possible attainment in anything you undertake.
11. Repeat this process as repetition builds habit.

Everything that we have is a result of this process. Everything. Be it good or bad, what we want or what we dislike. This process describes how our predominant mental attitude about everything is formed. Whether you like it or not, you are using this process. **Now that you know how this process works, you can use it consciously and of your own volition.**

Visualize what you want! Think big thoughts! To help you keep your goals in mind and not get distracted by lesser thoughts, it is highly recommended that you make for yourself a goal board. Here is a chance for you to have some fun with "arts & crafts."

Your Goal Board

Get for yourself a cork board or bulletin board. They can be bought at just about any store. You'll also need some thumb tacks or push pins. Finally, you'll need magazines or catalogues or 3x5 cards that have pictures or words describing the things that you want.

Go ahead! Get those items and then return to this exercise.

Here's where the fun begins. Clip pictures from the magazines or catalogues of the things that you want in your life. Perhaps you want a new car. Find a picture of the car you desire and snip it from the magazine and then post it onto your bulletin board. If you want to do something for which there is no picture, then write a brief description of it on a 3x5 card and post it. For example, you might write "I am the regional director of my company" on a card. You then post that card. It really helps if you get pictures of exactly what you want and not something "sort of like it." If you want your new car to be red, then get a picture of the car you want that is red.

When you assemble your goal board, hang it somewhere where you can easily see it, such as a wall near your desk. If you can, make a few goal boards and put them everywhere! This is very powerful and I have never seen it fail for people. When you look at your goal board, you will trigger your mind to think of those things that you want and set the law of attraction to work for you. When the Law is at work for you, nothing can keep the things away from you.

This method of using a goal board can help you attain your ideal weight. Here's how you do that. Find pictures of what you consider to be your ideal body. You might find something like that in a fitness magazine or a celebrity magazine. Who is your favourite movie star or celebrity? Surely you can find a picture of them.

Attain Your Ideal Weight

Next, you are to get a picture of yourself. Here's where the fun begins. Now you cut the head off the celebrity's picture and put your head there. You then take that composite and place it on your goal board.

What will happen is that you will visualize yourself with that body and you will then attract to yourself the events and conditions necessary for you to attain that ideal body and weight for yourself. Perhaps you will find yourself eating healthier or having more opportunities to get to the gym. Whatever the case, this method will help you get to your ideal weight.

A Key Point

There is no limit to what this law can do for you. Dare to believe in your own ideal. Remember that Nature is plastic to the ideal. Think of the ideal as an already accomplished fact.

Week Twenty-Two

Spiritual Seeds

*The Letter of
Transmittal*

In Week Twenty-Two you will find that thoughts are spiritual seeds, which, when planted in the subconscious mind, have a tendency to sprout and grow, but unfortunately the fruit is frequently not to our liking.

The various forms of inflammation, paralysis, nervousness, and diseased conditions generally are the manifestation of fear, worry, care, anxiety, jealousy, hatred, and similar thought.

The life processes are carried on by two distinct methods: First, the taking up and making use of nutritive material necessary for constructing cells; second, breaking down and excreting the waste material.

All life is based upon these constructive and destructive activities and as food, water, and air are the only requisites necessary for the construction of cells, it would seem that the problem of prolonging life indefinitely would not be a very difficult one.

However strange it may seem, it is the second or destructive activity that is, with rare exception, the cause of all disease. The waste material accumulates and saturates the tissues, which causes autointoxication. This may be partial or general. In the first case the disturbance will be local; in the second place it will affect the whole system.

The problem, then, before us in the healing of disease is to increase the inflow and distribution of vital energy throughout the system, and this can only be done by eliminating thoughts of fear, worry, care, anxiety, jealousy, hatred, and every other destructive thought, which tend to tear down and destroy the nerves and glands which control the excretion and elimination of poisonous and waste matter.

"Nourishing foods and strengthening tonics" cannot bestow life, because these are but secondary manifestations of life. The primary manifestation of life and how you may get in touch with it is explained in the part which I have the privilege of enclosing herewith.

Sickness may be eliminated by placing ourselves in harmony with Natural Law, which is Omnipotent.

The Main Points

A realization that man is a spiritual being and that this spirit must necessarily be perfect is the process of eliminating sickness.

A conscious recognition of this perfection, first intellectually, then emotionally, brings about a manifestation of this perfection.

This is so because thought is spiritual and therefore creative and correlates with its object and brings it into manifestation.

The Law of Vibration is brought into operation with this process.

This law governs because a higher rate of vibration governs, modifies, controls, changes, or destroys a lower rate of vibration.

There are over a million people in this country who make use of this system of mental therapeutics in one form or another.

The result of this system of thought is that for the first time in the world's history, every man's highest reasoning faculty can be satisfied by a demonstrable truth that is now fast flooding the world.

This system is applicable to other forms of supply as it will meet every human requirement or necessity.

This system is both scientific and religious. True science and religion are twin sisters. Where one goes, the other necessarily follows.

For your exercise this week concentrate on Tennyson's beautiful lines: "Speak to Him, thou, for He hears, and spirit with spirit can meet, Closer is He than breathing, and nearer than hands and feet." Then try to realize that when you do "Speak to Him" you are in touch with Omnipotence. This realization and recognition of this Omnipresent power will quickly destroy any and every form of sickness or suffering and substitute harmony and perfection. Then remember there are those who seem to think that sickness and suffering are sent by God; if so, every physician, every surgeon, and every Red Cross nurse is defying the will of God and hospitals and sanitariums are places of rebellion instead of houses of mercy. Of course, this quickly reasons itself into an absurdity, but there are many who still cherish the idea.

The Exercise

Then let the thought rest on the fact that until recently theology has been trying to teach an impossible Creator, one who created beings capable of sinning and then allowed them to be eternally punished for such sins. Of course the necessary outcome of such extraordinary ignorance was to create fear instead of love, and so, after two thousand years of this kind of propaganda, Theology is now busily engaged in apologizing for Christendom.

It's All On You

By now, I am certain that you realize that everything that you have in your life is because of your thoughts and those that you inherited. That puts what can be a huge burden on one's shoulders. It is the burden that you are responsible. It's your fault, whether it be for good or for bad.

What can be considered a huge burden, though, is in reality the greatest liberator in all of human history! Yes, you are responsible, but you can control what you have. The power is yours! You can use it just as you would a light switch or any machine. If it is dark where you are, then all you must do is flick a switch and turn on the light.

For no longer can you place the blame on anything or anyone else. It is now the time to look where you stand and take the reigns. That power is available for all and it does not have to be found or obtained. You already have it and it is within you. Claim it!

A Key Point

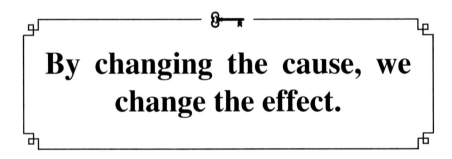

By changing the cause, we change the effect.

It Really Works.
Really.

Last week, you were shown a method by which you could attain your ideal weight or body type. Can you see now why this would work? Your brain and your thoughts set vibrations into motion that affect everything. What does Haanel say?

> When perfect images are placed before
> the subjective, the creative energies will
> build a perfect body.

What more can be said? If you have been doing the exercises and have not met with much success, then do them again. Reread the chapters and reapply the knowledge. The laws and ideas that Haanel espouses are absolute. They work perfectly.

your thoughts = your life

Leave the past behind you. Embrace the future and all of its possibilities. Allow yourself to unfold and enjoy the abundance that life provides.

As you have probably noticed, the exercises in *The Master Key System* are having you delve into your mind more and more. They build, one upon the other, so as to help you attain complete mental mastery. It is of the utmost importance that you follow and practice these exercises.

You Can Heal Your Life

As has been established, we are where we are in life because of our prior thoughts. Every thought we had, so long as we gave it power, became reality in our objective universe in one form or another. Your thoughts of worry or fear may have materialized in physical illness; thoughts of hate and envy perhaps in awkward social occasions; and all other ills that befell you had a precedent thought associated with it.

In her book, *You Can Heal Your Life*, Louise L. Hay lists common (and at times not so common) diseases and ailments and their associated probable mental cause. For example, for allergies, she has as the mental ailment, "Who are you allergic to?" She also includes a listing of affirmations that can be used to counteract the negative thought. Here is another example: For nervousness, she has listed as a probable cause "fear, anxiety...not trusting the life process." For the new thought pattern she would use to counteract it, she writes, "I am on an endless journey through eternity, and there is plenty of time. I communicate with my heart. All is well."

We bring forth that which we think. Study after study is showing that a patients mental attitude is just as important as the therapy administered. In some cases, a patient with a serious illness was cured by a placebo rather than a real drug or medicine!

When you sent love to the Universe, it most assuredly returned it. Strong, powerful, and courageous thoughts are returned to you in kind. They always have been. Think about the times you had a night on the town. What was your frame of mind when you made some new friends and enjoyed a lot of laughs? On the other hand, what was your frame of mind when you experienced not-so-nice people and had iffy experiences?

> It is the practical application that the value consists.

Many people subscribe to and try many different methods to better themselves. Unfortunately, many of the methods and attempts are exactly like fad diets — they provide temporary results, but do nothing for the long-term.

Keep Your Eyes on the Prize

Anything worth having is going to exact a price. *The Master Key System* is difficult at times. It demands of you to become your personal best. It takes time and practice. It will take some sweat, blood, and deep introspection. **The path is hard, but the rewards are commensurate with the effort.** Stay the course and keep practicing. This is your life and you are entitled to live it in the manner of your choosing. Live your dreams!

The Law of Love is a piece of pure science and the oldest and simplest form of Love is the elective affinity of two differing cells. Above all laws is the Law of Love, for Love is life.

—Charles F. Haanel,
Master Key Arcana

Week Twenty-Three

The Law of Success is Service

***The Letter of
Transmittal***

In the part which I have the honor to transmit herewith, you will find that money weaves itself into the entire fabric of our very existence; that the law of success is service; that we get what we give and for this reason we should consider it a great privilege to be able to give.

We have found that thought is the creative activity behind every constructive enterprise. We can therefore give nothing of more practical value than our thought.

Creative thought requires attention, and the power of attention is, as we have found, the weapon of the Super-man. Attention develops concentration, and concentration develops Spiritual Power, and Spiritual Power is the mightiest force in existence.

This is the science which embraces all sciences. It is the art which, above all arts, is relevant to human life. In the mastery of this science and this art there is opportunity for unending progression. Perfection in this is not acquired in six days, or in six weeks, or in six months. It is the labor of a life. Not to go forward is to go backward.

It is inevitable that the entertainment of positive, constructive, and unselfish thoughts should have a far-reaching effect for good. Compensation is the keynote of the universe. Nature is constantly seeking to strike an equilibrium. Where something is sent out, something must be received, else there should be a vacuum formed. By observance of this rule you cannot fail to profit in such measure as to amply justify your effort along this line.

The first law of success is service.   ***The Main Points***

We may be of the most service by having an open mind. By being interested
    in the race rather than the goal, in the pursuit rather than possession.

Selfish thought contains the germs of dissolution.

Our greatest success will be achieved by a recognition of the fact that it is
    just as essential to give as to receive.

Financiers frequently meet with great success because they do their own
    thinking.

The great majority in every country remain docile and apparently willing
    tools of the few because they let the few do all their thinking for them.

The effect of concentrating upon sorrow and loss is more sorrow and loss.

The effect of concentrating upon gain is more gain.

This is the only principle that is ever used, or ever can be used, in the busi-
    ness world. There is no other principle. That fact that it may be used un-
    consciously does not alter or change the situation.

The practical application of this principle is the fact that success is an ef-
    fect, not a cause, and if we wish to secure the effect we must ascertain the
    cause or idea or thought by which the effect is created.

This week concentrate on the fact that man is not a body with a spirit, but a   ***The Exercise***
spirit with a body, and that it is for this reason that his desires are incapable
of any permanent satisfaction in anything not spiritual. Money is therefore
of no value except to bring about the conditions which we desire and these
conditions are necessarily harmonious. Harmonious conditions necessitate
sufficient supply, so that if there appears to be any lack, we should realize
that the idea—or soul—of money is service, and as this thought takes form,
channels of supply will be opened and you will have the satisfaction of
knowing that spiritual methods are entirely practical.

Economics

When an exchange of value for value is made, then one has balance. That means that when we trade or buy something, we are putting the law of balances to work. Someone has something that you want and you have something he wants. All that is needed is an agreement on the price.

You can enjoy abundance simply by earning more than you are spending. As Haanel states, the first law of success is service.

A Key Point

> **We make money by making friends, and we enlarge our circle of friends by making money for them, by helping them, by being of service to them. The first law of success is service, and this in turn is built on integrity and justice.**

You Scratch My Back...

Helping friends or people to make money does not mean be charitable. It does mean that you participate in the economic system. Look at the bills a business owner must pay! From rent to sundry suppliers to payroll, he is a veritable cornucopia of money. **If he is thinking, though, the dollars he spends return to him.**

Throughout this book, you have looked at yourself and made many lists about yourself. You should put all of those to good use. What can you do that would be of service to others? The founder of IBM, Thomas J. Watson Sr., made a single word the company motto:

THINK

Thought may be the only thing that you have at the moment. It will always be the most valuable thing that you own. **A labourer has a wage that has a cap, because the physical body has bounds; a thinker knows no bounds because the Mind is in touch with the Infinite.**

One idea can change the world. One idea can net for you millions of dollars. Look around you and realize that everything that you have came from somewhere and that everything originated in the mind. Someone's mind envisioned and planned what you are using, sitting on, watching, eating.

Never before has it been more possible to realize your idea. Production costs are decreasing, the Internet has become a viable medium, and knowledge and information are everywhere. **We are in the midst of a great Renaissance. Take advantage of everything. Think!**

Week Twenty-Four

Alchemy

***The Letter of
Transmittal***

Enclosed herewith you will find Week Twenty-Four. This is the final lesson.

If you have practiced each of the exercises a few minutes every day, as suggested, you will have found that you can get out of life exactly what you wish by first putting into life that which you wish, and you will probably agree with the student who said: "The thought is almost overwhelming, so vast, so available, so definite, so reasonable, and so usable."

The fruit of this knowledge is, as it were, a gift of the Gods. It is the "truth" that makes men free—not only free from every lack and limitation, but free from sorrow, worry, and care, and is it not wonderful to realize that this law is no respecter of persons, that it makes no difference what your habit of thought may be? The way has been prepared.

If you are inclined to be religious, the greatest religious teacher the world has ever known made the way so plain that all may follow. If your mental bias is toward physical science, the law will operate with mathematical certainty. If you are inclined to be philosophical, Plato or Emerson may be your teacher, but in either case, you may reach degrees of power to which it is impossible to assign any limit.

An understanding of this principle, I believe, is the secret for which the ancient Alchemists vainly sought, because it explains how gold in the mind may be transmuted into gold in the heart and in the hand.

The Main Points

The theory and practice of every system of Metaphysics in existence depend upon a knowledge of the Truth" concerning yourself and the world in which you live.

The "Truth" concerning yourself is that the real "I" or ego is spiritual and can therefore never be less than perfect.

To destroy any form of error, you are to absolutely convince yourself of the "Truth" concerning the condition that you wish to see manifested.

The Universal Mind in which "we live and move and have our being" is one and indivisible, it is therefore just as possible to help others as to help ourselves.

The Universal Mind is the totality of all mind in existence.

The Universal Mind is omnipresent, it exists everywhere. There is no place where it is not. It is therefore within us. It is "The world within." It is our spirit, our life.

The nature of the Universal Mind is that it is spiritual and consequently creative. It seeks to express itself in form.

Our ability to think is our ability to act on the Universal Mind and bring it into manifestation for the benefit of ourselves and others.

Thinking is clear, decisive, calm, deliberate, sustained thought with a definite end in view.

The result of thinking is that you will also be able to say, "It is not I that doeth the works, but the 'Father' that dwelleth within me. He doeth the works." You will come to know that the "Father" is the Universal Mind and that He does really and truly dwell within you. In other words, you will come to know that the wonderful promises made in the Bible are fact, not fiction, and can be demonstrated by anyone having sufficient understanding.

The Exercise

This week, try to realize that this is truly a wonderful world in which we live, that you are a wonderful being, that many are awakening to a knowledge of the Truth, and as fast as they awake and come into a knowledge of the "things which have been prepared for them" they, too, realize that "Eye hath not seen, nor ear heard, neither hath it entered into the heart of man," the splendors which exist for those who find themselves in the Promised Land. They have crossed the river of judgment and have arrived at the point of discrimination between the true and the false, and have found that all they ever willed or dreamed was but a faint concept of the dazzling reality.

The Road Ahead

You now have within your possession The Master Key. You now know that there are no secrets or mysteries. There is merely the fact that you must realize your possession of the Key and take it.

Everything is possible. With your mind and your thinking, you can dream any dream and have it become reality.

Continue to practice the exercises, those contained in both The Master Key System and in this Workbook. Train yourself with the utmost discipline and persistence. Remember what Haanel says about the mind.

> When man's mind is made perfect, then—and then only—will the body be able perfectly to express itself.

Find new and other books to read. Continuously feed your mind. Delve into the books that are listed at the end of this Workbook. Reading is a source of inspiration, ideas, knowledge, entertainment, and information. Often, a person gets caught up in reading things that do not feed the mind properly. He will spend his time reading every newspaper, but not a spare minute for real mental food. Here is how you can model your reading habits for peak effect.

Self-Help/Inspiration	**35%**
Education/Knowledge	**30%**
Newspapers/Information	**15%**
Entertainment	**20%**

If we whittle away our time by reading slop, then we run the risk of ruining the best and only tool that we have. That is not to say that we should neglect our entertainment, but let's face facts, some people only tend to their entertainment wants to the exclusion of everything else. Also, while it is fine and well to be informed about current events, there comes a point when getting information is akin to gossiping. Know the difference.

By any means, you should continue to read books from which you can become educated. If you own a business, then read books about tax methods. Are you a writer? Then it would do you well to read books on style. Brush up your math skills. What is the nature of quantum reality? We live in a world where information flows like water. Knowledge pours into our lives from every corner. Fill your glass with it.

As you think, thus you will do. The brain leads and the body follows. We think and then we do. That should be obvious by now and ingrained into your psyche. All that is left is for you to put it into operation for yourself. I urge you to continue on this journey. Once you set this into motion, stopping would be the worst thing you can do. Live your life and live your dreams!

A human being should be able to change a diaper, plan an invasion, butcher a hog, design a building, conn a ship, write a sonnet, balance accounts, build a wall, set a bone, comfort the dying, take orders, give orders, cooperate, act alone, solve an equation, analyze a new problem, pitch manure, program a computer, cook a tasty meal, fight efficiently, die gallantly. Specialization is for insects.

—Robert A. Heinlein

Man is ignorant of the nature of his own being and powers. Even his idea of his limitations is based on experience of the past. There is therefore no reason to assign theoretical limits to what he may be, or what he may do.

—Aleister Crowley, *Magick*

Guard your thoughts well, for what you really are in your secret thoughts today, be it good or evil, you will, sooner or later, become in actual deed.

—James Allen, "Thought and Action"
from *Master Key Arcana*

There's only one corner of the universe you can be certain of improving and that's your own self.

—Aldous Huxley

People who are unable to motivate themselves must be content with mediocrity, no matter how impressive their other talents.

—Andrew Carnegie

The Last Words

Great minds have purpose, others have wishes.

—Washington Irving

Do not find fault; find a remedy.

—Henry Ford

As a man thinks in his heart, so is he.

—King Solomon

The person who makes a success of living is the one who sees his goal steadily and aims for it unswervingly. That is dedication.

—Cecil B. DeMille

Make no little plans; they have no magic to stir men's blood…make big plans, aim high in hope and work.

—Daniel H. Burnham

He who has a "why" to live for can bear almost any "how."

—Friedrich Nietzsche

Circumstances—what are circumstances? I make circumstances.

—Napoleon Bonaparte

Your garden is not complete until there's nothing more you can take out of it.

—Japanese Proverb

Additional Reading List

Books published by Kallisti Publishing...

The Amazing Secrets of the Yogi	Charles F. Haanel
Master Key Arcana	Charles F. Haanel
Size Matters!	MiMi Paris
Getting Connected Through Exceptional Leadership	Karl Walinskas

A list of some of the best books ever written in alphabetical order by title...

The Art of War	Sun Tzu
Atlas Shrugged	Ayn Rand
Be Here Now	Baba Ram Dass
The Holographic Universe	Michael Talbot
How To Get Rich on Other People's Money	Tyler G. Hicks
How To Make Your Daydreams Come True	Elmer Wheeler
In Search of the Miraculous	P.D. Ouspensky
Innovation and Entrepreneurship	Peter F. Drucker
The Lazy Man's Way to Riches	Richard G. Nixon
The Mafia Manager	Lee Wallek
The Magic of Believing	Claude M. Bristol
Mathemagics	Arthur Benjamin & Michael Shermer
Meta-Physics: New Dimensions of the Mind	Anthony Norvell
The Millionaire's Secret	Mark Fisher
No Rules: 21 Giant Lies About Success	Dan S. Kennedy
Prometheus Rising	Robert Anton Wilson
Psycho Cybernetics	Maxwell Maltz
Psycho Pictography	Vernon Howard
The Pure Joy of Making More Money	Donald M. Dible
Rhinoceros Success	Scott Alexander
A Rich Man's Secret	Ken Roberts
The Richest Man in Babylon	George S. Clason
Science and Health	Mary Baker Eddy
The Secret of the Ages	Robert Collier
Self-Reliance and Other Essays	Ralph Waldo Emerson
The Story of Civilization	Will & Ariel Durant
The Success System That Never Fails	W. Clement Stone
Super-Learning	Sheila Ostrander & Lynn Schroeder
Think & Grow Rich	Napoleon Hill
The Venture	Jeff Cox
The Way of Strategy	William A. Levinson
You Were Born Rich	Bob Proctor
you^2	Price Pritchett, Ph.D.
Zen Flesh, Zen Bones	Paul Reps

This is not a complete or comprehensive list by any means, but it is a good list with which to start. Every one of these books is well worth reading. Hopefully, they will lead you to new successes.

When I get a little money I buy books; and if any is left I buy food and clothes.

—Erasmus

Great books from Kallisti Publishing...

"What a wonderful book. It is truly a guide to live by. When I picked it up, I read it from cover to cover. Since that time, I have read each chapter again several times. The words of the author come from a person who has lived what she talks about. I thoroughly enjoyed and benefited from this terrific book."

Size Matters!
MiMi Paris

$11.95

"This book was a breath of fresh air, a much needed interlude between your average long-winded, short-sensed leadership guides. The author has a knack for keeping you entertained, while pointing out strengths and weaknesses of your average leader. I would definitely recommend picking up this book..."

Getting Connected Through Exceptional Leadership
Karl Walinskas

$13.95

"This is one of the more interesting books I have read on the topic of yoga. I love that it really explores the power of breath and discusses techniques to harness prana. Many recent books tend to skim over this aspect of yoga, but Haanel really devoted himself to this very powerful practice."

The Amazing Secrets of the Yogi
Charles F. Haanel

$18.95

"I just received my copy of *Master Key Arcana*. Thanks for the really fast service. This book is sure to become a classic."

Master Key Arcana
Charles F. Haanel

$17.95

Use this order form...

U se this Order Form to purchase additional books from Kallisti Publishing. Books make great gifts (for both yourself and others) and all of Kallisti's books are guaranteed to make a positive impact in anybody's life.

In order to ensure that you receive the quickest service:

> 1. Indicating the quantity you would like.
> 2. Compute the total price.
> 3. Compute shipping costs.
> 4. Add the total cost of the books and the shipping costs.
> 5. Include cheque or money order when you send your order.
> 6. Send order to:
>
> **Kallisti Publishing**
> **332 Center Street**
> **Wilkes-Barre, PA 18702**

Book	Quan-tity	Price	Total
The Master Key System		**$19.95**	
Master Key Arcana		**$17.95**	
The Amazing Secrets of the Yogi		**$18.95**	
The Master Key Work-book		**$29.95**	
Size Matters!		**$11.95**	
Getting Connected Through Exceptional Leadership		**$13.95**	
Road Map for National Security: Imperative for Change		**$18.95**	

Shipping and handling: 1-5 books $4.95	**Shipping**		
6-10 books $6.95 11-20 books $8.95	**Total**		**$**

Shipping and handling:
1-5 books $4.95
6-10 books $6.95
11-20 books $8.95
Add .50 for each additional book.
These rates apply to the U.S. only.

Name _____

Address _____

City/State/Zip _____

Phone/Email _____

Send order to: Kallisti Publishing, 332 Center Street, Wilkes-Barre, PA 18702
Allow one to two weeks for delivery. Prices and availability subject to change without notice.

Mindset to Millionaire

Kallisti Publishing and Bob Schmitz
are proud to present
Bob Schmitz's *Mindset to Millionaire*!

It has been almost ten years since Bob Schmitz presented his famous *Mindset to Millionaire* series of seminars. Luckily, they were preserved on audio tape and are now available on high-quality audio CD!

The *Mindset to Millionaire* seminars influenced thousands of people to use their minds to accumulate the wealth and position in life that they wanted. Businesses and organizations bought the original tape set by the dozens so that their representatives and sales forces could benefit from one of the most powerful audio programs ever developed. For the first time in many years, you, too, can benefit!

While listening to this 70+ minute CD, you will hear and learn:

> **~The best ways to set goals to achieve maximum results.**
> **~Why bad things happen to good people—and how you can**
> **avoid the bad while still being good.**
> **~How your attitude determines your "altitude".**
> **~What you should be thinking rather than what you should**
> **be doing. (Hint: The brain leads, the body follows!)**
> **~And much, much more.**

Bob Schmitz, who is the co-author of *The Master Key Workbook*, presents all of the information in a way that only Bob can do. He is funny, instructive, and most of all, precise. This is one audio CD you definitely should own so that you can listen to it again and again as you think your way to the life that you deserve and desire.

It would have cost you quite a bit of money to attend one of Bob's *Mindset to Millionaire* seminars. Even if you could track down one of the tape sets today, it would be difficult to pry it from the owner's hands. Thankfully, you don't have to worry about such things. You can begin *thinking* your way to wealth for only $16.95. This program is so good, it is backed by an **unconditional money-back guarantee**!

Order *Mindset to Millionaire* today!
www.mindsettomillionaire.com

Here are some web sites that you should bookmark and visit frequently.

www.kallistipublishing.com

www.themasterkeyinstitute.com

www.charlesfhaanel.com

www.masterkeycoaching.com

www.masterkeyworkbook.com

Thank you very much. As always, be kind and have fun!